MW01515891

DIDN'T
SEE THAT
COMING

WHEN HOW THEY'RE LIVING'S
NOT HOW YOU RAISED THEM

ENDORSEMENTS

As a senior pastor of a church with a few thousand members, I can truthfully say a river of tears runs from my office whose depths resemble the Congo River. It comes from the hurt, embarrassment, and pain of post-modern parents who know what it feels like to give their children the best of everything and then watch those same kids take awkward turns and wicked twists pushing them to shout, "Didn't see that coming!"

Esteemed author and parental cohort Dr. Sharon Elliott has placed her hand of compassion and wisdom on the slender nerve so many parents secretly want someone to touch. It is what makes this book a must read. If you have children, grandchildren, or even great-grandkids get this work and give it your sincere and devout attention. Its stories are real, its issues are relevant, its truths are life-changing and its resolutions are truly redemptive.

Dr. Elliott's books are always awesome; however, she is simply ingenious in this work.

—Dr. John R. Adolph, Senior Pastor, Antioch Missionary Baptist Church, Beaumont, Texas

Didn't See That Coming: When How They're Living's Not How You Raised Them is a heart provoking how-to guide for parenting our adult children, and Dr. Sharon Norris Elliott has hit this one out the park. She has captured parents' messy thoughts and feelings about their adult children who are not only making some of the same mistakes we made but are also creating some disturbing new ones. I wish this book had been available when I was dealing with my reluctant-to-tell-us LGBTQ daughter; however, Sharon's down-to-earth approach to stories and Scripture has inspired me to pick up the tools of compassion, courage, and "care-frontation." *Didn't See That Coming* encourages us and shows us how to never give up on our adult children, because no matter what, God will never give up on them or us.

—Lady Laura Simon, pastor's wife, women's leader, Covenant City Fellowship, Santa Ana,

Didn't See That Coming is full of nuggets you can use to enrich your life. I encourage every parent to read this book as you navigate through the challenges of parenting. Dr. Sharon Norris Elliott reaches out through the pages of this book with practical wisdom designed to equip parents to stand in love on the foundation of Scripture when your adult kids are not living how they were raised. Refreshing and inspirational, I highly recommend you pick up a copy of *Didn't See That Coming* for yourself and all your acquaintances who have grown children.

—Rev. Welton Pleasant, II, president of the California State Baptist Convention, vice-president of the Far West Region of the National Baptist Convention, senior pastor of Christ Second Baptist Church, Long Beach, California

Dr. Sharon Norris Elliott has created a roadmap to help make a hurting parent's journey easier to travel. Not only will she show you are not alone, but she will also share her own stories as well as the stories of other hurting parents. She has the clarity to help you understand your situation not only biblically, but with a heart of love. Among many other vital helps in *Didn't See That Coming,* Dr. Sharon will give you prayers to pray and shows you how to press into God as you learn to parent in difficult situations.

—Linda Evans Shepherd, Founder of Advanced Writers and Speakers Association**,** author of *Prayers for Every Need*

DIDN'T
SEE THAT
COMING

WHEN HOW THEY'RE LIVING'S
NOT HOW YOU RAISED THEM

DR. SHARON NORRIS ELLIOTT

ELK LAKE PUBLISHING INC

PUBLISHING THE POSITIVE
Plymouth, Massachusetts

A Christian Company
ElkLakePublishingInc.com

COPYRIGHT NOTICE

Didn't See That Coming: When How They're Living's Not How You Raised Them

First edition. Copyright © 2023 by Sharon Norris Elliott. The information contained in this book is the intellectual property of Sharon Norris Elliott and is governed by United States and International copyright laws. All rights reserved. No part of this publication, either text or image, may be used for any purpose other than personal use. Therefore, reproduction, modification, storage in a retrieval system, or retransmission, in any form or by any means, electronic, mechanical, or otherwise, for reasons other than personal use, except for brief quotations for reviews or articles and promotions, is strictly prohibited without prior written permission by the publisher.

Unless otherwise indicated Scripture taken from the New King James Version®. Copyright 1982 by Thomas Nelson. Used by permission. All rights reserved.

Scripture quotations marked MSG are taken from *THE MESSAGE*, copyright 1993, 2002, 2018 by Eugene H. Peterson.

Scripture quotations marked NLT are taken from the *Holy Bible*, New Living Translation, copyright © 1996, 2004, 2015 by Tyndale House Foundation.

Scripture quotations marked TLB are taken from The Living Bible copyright © 1971 by Tyndale House Foundation.

Scripture quotations marked (CEV) are from the Contemporary English Version Copyright © 1991, 1992, 1995 by American Bible Society. Used by Permission.

Scripture quotations marked TPT are from The Passion Translation®. Copyright © 2017, 2018, 2020 by Passion & Fire Ministries, Inc.

Scripture quotations marked KJV are from the King James Versions. Public domain.

Cover and Interior Design: Amber Weingand-Buckley, Derinda Babcock, Deb Haggerty
Editor(s): Peggy Ellis, Judy Hagey, Susan K. Stewart, Deb Haggerty

Author Represented By: Jevon Bolden, Embolden Media Group

PUBLISHED BY: Elk Lake Publishing, Inc., 35 Dogwood Drive, Plymouth, MA 02360, 2020

Library Cataloging Data

Names: Elliott, Sharon Norris (Sharon Norris Elliott)

Didn't See That Coming: When How They're Living's Not How You Raised Them/ Sharon Norris Elliot

224 p. 23cm × 15cm (9 in. × 6 in.)

ISBN-13: 978-1-64949-780-2 (paperback) | 978-1-64949-781-9 (trade hardcover) | 978-1-64949-782-6 (trade paperback) | 978-1-64949-783-3 (e-book)

Key Words: Christian parenting, parenting adults (adult children), parent-child relationships, understanding adult children, how to parent adult children, adult children's issues

Library of Congress Control Number: 2022951286 Nonfiction

DEDICATION

To Matthew and Mark:

- The babies who heard my heartbeat from the inside.
- The toddlers who gave me so many laughs and smiles.
- The young boys who attended church regularly, were baptized, and expressed a personal confession of faith.
- The preteens who went through elementary and middle school without a hitch.
- The teenagers who enjoyed and made the most of high school.
- The college men who pursued and earned their bachelor's degrees.
- The men: Mark who is an amazing husband and father; Matthew who has allowed his talents to carve a significant place in the world; and both who are founders and CEOs of their own companies, continuing through life as believers in Christ, productive members of society, and their momma's pride and joy.

I may not have seen some things coming, but I would not have wanted to miss one nanosecond of being your mom. You are a major reason why God put me on this planet and why I can go on every day. I love you one more than you can say all day!

TABLE OF CONTENTS

FOREWORD

FOREWORD BY PAM FARREL

Do you have a life-giving friend? Someone you can be raw and real with? Someone who speaks truth and hope into your mind? A friend who is so filled with biblical wisdom and good common-sense the fog lifts, and the sun shines through to enlighten your next step on the uphill climb you find yourself on? Sharon Elliott is that kind of friend.

We all need the kind of mentor Mary, the mother of Jesus, found in Elizabeth. Mary, a teen mother, likely had many overwhelming feelings. She knew the baby inside her was holy, but she needed wisdom to walk out the journey ahead, so she went to her older and wiser cousin. Read Luke 1:39–45 aloud to capture the powerful and positive greeting wrapped in wisdom Elizabeth gave Mary:

> At the time Mary got ready and hurried to a town in the hill country of Judea, where she entered Zechariah's home and greeted Elizabeth. When Elizabeth heard Mary's greeting, the baby leaped in her womb, and Elizabeth was filled with the Holy Spirit. In a loud voice she exclaimed: "Blessed are you among women and blessed is the child you will bear! But why am I so favored, that the mother of my Lord should come to me? As soon as the sound of your greeting reached my ears, the baby in my womb leaped for joy. Blessed

is she who has believed that the Lord would fulfill his promises to her!" (TLB)

My life is a series of mentor moments strung together like a lovely pearl necklace. Kathy was a woman who saw the chaos of a home filled with the rage of an alcoholic dad, so Kathy invited us to church and brought our family to Jesus. Tina, a staff member of Cru, only five years older than me, poured a solid spiritual foundation into my life so instead of repeating dysfunctional family patterns, I recognized a godly and good-hearted man, Bill, who soon would be my husband.

When God called us to attend seminary, this country girl was stunned at the thought of living in urban Los Angeles, so I cried all night, until my husband recommended I talk to an older wiser woman. I thought of Barbara. Her husband was in the oil business, so at one point, her entire family was called to move to the Middle East, to a nation hostile to Americans, Christians, and women—but she and her marriage and family thrived for many years despite the environment. I called Barbara and asked if she would have time to talk with me. I rode my bike to her home after my hours as a high school special ed aide. Barbara began to recount the faithfulness of God in her life, then she and her husband took me to dinner, and they continued to recount the faithfulness of God in their lives, then they took me for ice cream, and she continued to recount the faithfulness of God, and as I waited for my new husband to come pick me up, Barbara prayed the faithfulness of God into my life. That night, as Bill and I walked through their front door, I was convinced I could walk through *any* door God opened because HE is faithful!

If we are unfaithful, he remains faithful, for he cannot deny who he is (2 Timothy 2:13 NLT).

Then I became a mother, and Nora, a mother of four godly children, two in our youth group, tucked me under her wing and shared how to become a godly mom. Janeen, a teaching leader with Bible Study Fellowship (BSF), poured God's truth into my heart, mostly over extended family meals, free haircuts, and pool time. As we headed to seminary, Phoebe, the seminary president's wife, taught me what a pastor's wife could become.

Then I hit my first mommy-life speed bump. Our middle son was ADD-ADHD, and I needed new methods to parent him (and survive his antics!) I began to interview every mom of a strong-willed, special-need, and hyperactive child I knew. So many of these moms were women of prayer, so I joined *Moms in Prayer* to meet even more of these wise, godly, and practical mothers. I gathered relationships and friendships with as many overcoming mothers as I could find. And it was providential, because when my middle son hit a rough patch early in college and was drifting from God into prodigal waters, I needed, and he needed, the prayers, commonsense advice, and hope they held out to me and our family.

Through all my years as a pastor's wife, a director of women's ministry, and mother, I kept praying, "Lord, there needs to be one book to encapsulate all the many issues and problems ever growing in society which are impacting families and children today. Lord, we need the path to kick Satan to the curb and crush his attacks. Lord, we, your people, need your truth, your wisdom, your love, and your compassion. Your people need your words to speak freedom and triumph into our children and our friends' children."

Sharon Elliott is a life-giving, victorious, biblical strong, yet amazingly compassionate friend who is answering the prayer. The wisdom on these pages is like having coffee with a best friend. The pages are filled with powerful

Scriptures to address some of the most challenging issues a mom can face in the world today. Sharon has gathered real life illustrations and insight from other parents who have walked out God's ways with their prodigals to the best of their abilities. Sharon has also assembled verses from God's Word on all these exceedingly difficult circumstances plus personalized prayers you can pray over your children or the prodigals of your friends and family. I also love Sharon's amazing balance between truth and love in her "Care-frontation" sections, because often in a parent's challenging moments, the best words to open or traverse conversations with our teen or young adult kids can feel hard to come by. Sharon and the sensible troop of godly parents who contributed to this helpful and hopeful book give us a way forward. Sharon has even added a dash of humor because on those dark or difficult days, Lord knows we need a smile to lighten our heavy load.

One of my favorite phrases in this entire power-packed, skillfully written, prayerfully woven book is, "When God is honored, he has a way of making our mess-ups turn into miracles."

I saw God give our family guardrails to our journey with our prodigal, who has become a God-honoring leader. Cry out to God, pick up this book, and look inside for your next step.

Take hold of the verses of hope, like:

> But Jesus looked at them and said, "With men this is impossible, but with God all things are possible." (Matthew 19:26)

> "Ah, Lord God! Behold, You have made the heavens and the earth by Your great power and outstretched arm. There is nothing too hard for You." (Jeremiah 32:17)

> Fear not, for I *am* with you; be not dismayed, for I *am* your God. I will strengthen you, yes, I will help you, I

will uphold you with My righteous right hand. (Isaiah 41:10)

My soul, wait silently for God alone, for my expectation *is* from Him. He only *is* my rock and my salvation; *He is* my defense; I shall not be moved. (Psalm 62:5–6)

Turn the page. Hope is ahead. Help is on the way.

Pam Farrel

- "The one who gets wisdom loves life." (Proverbs 19:8)
- Author of over fifty books including bestselling *Men Are Like Waffles, Women Are Like Spaghetti, 10 Best Decisions a Parent Can Make* and co-author of *Discovering Hope in the Psalms: A Creative Bible Study Experience.*
- Co-Director of *Love-Wise* Ministry.
- Married to Bill forty-two years, Mom to three sons, three daughters-in-law, and Nana to five grandchildren who all are currently walking with Jesus.

ACKNOWLEDGMENTS

For this and every book I ever write, I am indebted to:

The Holy Trinity; my parents, Vincent and Nancy Norris; my husband, James Elliott; my children and grandchildren; my extended family; my pastor, Rev. Welton Pleasant, II; and my friends.

The legacy left to me, and confidence built into me by my parents have formed a solid foundation under my life, which continues to hold me up and drive me forward. The love of God and all these people keep me encouraged to continue to write what God has put on my heart.

I am thankful beyond expression for being surrounded by their care, concern, wisdom, listening ears, laughter, and even shoulders to cry on when necessary.

DEAR READER,

Like you, I am a parent of adult children. Bravo to you parents who are reading this book in advance of facing the issues herein; however, I particularly want to be sure you know I'm walking alongside those of you who have said from time to time, "Oh Lord, I didn't see that coming! They are not living the way I raised them!" What's a parent to do?

Be assured, you are not alone in your journey with your young adult. Christian families are not exempt from trauma. Just because parents raise their kids in church, pray over them constantly, and live before them consistently, doesn't necessarily mean the children will grow up and always make godly, righteous choices for their lives.

So, to let you know even more definitively you are not alone, each chapter begins with "Similar Chronicles"—one or two stories from parents who are facing, or who have faced, the issue being discussed. My stories, as well as the situations submitted by others are true, but the names and some other identifying features in most of the accounts have been changed to protect the privacy of the individuals involved.

This book is more than a misery-loves-company collection of stories by whiny parents mad at their grown kids for messing up. Very real comfort can be gained from knowing you are not the only Christian parents who have ever faced these issues with your adult child. This book explains each issue ("Stressful Complication"), makes clear what God's word says about the matter ("Savior's Communication"), and suggests ways to interject both love and truth into the situation ("Sincere Care-frontation"). Pay special attention to the word "care-frontation" as opposed to confrontation. It is my desire and prayer we tenderly communicate our love for our children while we courageously share wisdom and truth with them. Tenderness and courage equal compassion and empathy and that's positive care-frontation rather than negative confrontation.

Every chapter then ends with prayer ("Sweet Communion") and a list of resources you can turn to for even more help ("Supportive Connections").

Happy reading!

Ablaze, Sharon

—CHAPTER 1—
INVITATION TO BELIEVE

"Mom and Dad, would you still love me no matter what I told you?"

And so begin conversations leading to next sentences we never saw coming. We brace ourselves. Angst flows as a damaging undertow, sometimes swirling for years, bubbles to the surface through our child's words. The confessions reveal news we just don't want to hear. We feel our blood pressure soaring; our heartbeats must be audible. *Please stop*, our brains cry. *But keep talking*, our hearts counter. We struggle to stay calm, conceal the frowns, and blink back the tears. All at once, the questions and thoughts crash through like lightning bolts:

- Are you serious?
- How could this be when you were raised in church?
- Our family doesn't have this problem.
- Don't you know what the Bible says about this?
- We've failed as parents.
- What could we have done differently?
- Why?

Fear. Confusion. Shame. Embarrassment. Isolation. Disbelief. Helplessness. The knot in the pit of our stomachs tightens and won't go away. We realize we're not perfect, but we did everything we knew to do to raise this child right. Now this adult child is standing in front of us, or talking to us on the phone, saying the unthinkable.

"I'm pregnant."

"I'm leaving the church."

"I'm dropping out of school."

"Can you come pick me up? I'm at the downtown jail about to be locked up."

"I need some money. I thought my win at the card table was a sure bet."

"I'm getting divorced."

"I need a ride because I lost my license on a DUI (Driving Under the Influence).

"I'm gay."

Throughout time, parents have watched from the sidelines as their adult children entered into troubling circumstances. Even after the Father God supplied his first children, Adam and Eve, with absolutely everything they needed, they disobeyed, insisting upon going after the one thing they didn't need. The result? Hard work and labor pains. Yes, mankind is still suffering the consequences of the original Eden garden debacle. If God had trouble with his very first children, what chance do we think we have of avoiding a similar fate with ours?

The second set of biblical children didn't learn from their parents' mistake either. Son A ended up murdering Son B, and then Son A got ostracized by society, leaving the parents bereft of both sons. (See Genesis chapters 3 and 4 for details on the aforementioned accounts.)

Today's distinct problems may be different, but the desperate circumstances are exactly the same. We parents ache over the mistakes, misjudgments, faults, failures, shocking decisions, and shameful deeds of our kids. When they were small and got themselves into trouble, we could slap a bandage on the boo-boo, apply the board of education to the seat of knowledge, or send them to their room with the command they simply "cut that out." But now they're grown, and neither their issues nor our solutions are as simple. Consider how some long-ago parents handled the serious problems their children faced:

SCENE ONE

It was atypical and seemed out of character for Jairus, one of the rulers of the synagogue, to approach Jesus, not as a prominent person, but as a desperate dad. As the ever-growing throng pressed in on the young rabbi with the reported power to dispel diseases, Jairus's presence and request stood out as even more unusual. He didn't habitually mingle with the common people, but his current dilemma overrode his social preferences. Yes, he'd heard Jesus had cured some illnesses, but could he fulfill Jairus's request to reverse the ultimatum of death, which hung threateningly over his twelve-year-old daughter?

"My little daughter lies at the point of death. Come and lay your hands on her, that she may be healed, and she will live." The crowd thronging Jesus paused in disbelief as this synagogue ruler—one to whom everyone else came for assistance and advice—threw himself at Jesus's feet, beseeching help from this compassionate street preacher.

Jesus neither shied away from the request nor suspected ulterior motives. He saw only a frantic father with a desperate need, so he simply went with Jairus, as did the curious, look-y-loo crowd. In route, Jairus received the message his little girl had died and there was no need to bring Jesus after all. However, Jesus told him, "Do not be afraid; only believe." When Jesus got to Jairus's house, he raised the little girl (See Mark 5:22–23, 35–36).

SCENE TWO

A Canaanite woman approached Jesus begging him to heal her demon-possessed daughter. The disciples were incensed by the intrusion of this foreign woman, and at first, it seemed as though Jesus felt the same way. Initially, Jesus ignored her. Even after she drew near to him in worship, he informed her he was only sent to the Jews and not to the dogs (that's what Jews called Canaanites and Samaritans). But her mission would not be thwarted. She answered, "Truth, Lord: yet the dogs eat of the crumbs which fall from their masters' table." Jesus then responded, "O woman, great *is* your faith! Let it be to you as you desire." Then he healed her daughter (See Matthew 15:21–28).

SCENE THREE

A distressed father struggled to get his demon-possessed, deaf, and mute son to the disciples for healing. When it became apparent the disciples were unsuccessful, the man petitioned Jesus. Since the boy had been suffering in this state since childhood, the father begged Jesus saying, "If you can do anything, have compassion on us and help us." Jesus told the man, "If you can believe, all things *are* possible to him who believes." To this, the father of the young man immediately cried out with tears, "Lord, I believe; help my unbelief!" Then Jesus delivered the boy (See Mark 9:21–24).

A little girl raised, a young lady healed, a young man delivered—these three scenes show us several truths.

First, one's station in life does not matter when it comes to concern for the welfare of one's children. Jairus was probably pretty well off, whereas the Canaanite woman and the father could have been average wage earners. Jairus was well-respected; the woman was considered "a dog." We may all come from different walks of life, but hospital waiting rooms, jail holding tanks, and mental health facilities are great equalizers. All parents want their children to be healthy and whole, and when they are not, we will go to the ends of the earth (and the ends of our bank accounts) to make them well.

Second, political correctness doesn't matter when considering the welfare of our children. People would have been surprised to see Jairus asking Jesus for a favor. Talk about opposite parties; it seemed as if they would have been at opposite poles. Many synagogue rulers acted as if they should be treated as gods, and here Jesus was walking around claiming to *be* God. By approaching Jesus like this in public, Jairus ignored the opinions of many of his colleagues. The Canaanite woman would never have barged in on a group of men, yet there she was in the midst of Jesus and his disciples, bearing up under their dismissive attitudes because her daughter's need was more important than their disdain. The father didn't give up after the disciples' failure to heal his son. Without another thought, he went over their heads to *their* Master seeking the help he needed for his son.

Whatever issues our children are facing, we too must determine we will not be stopped in the interest of political correctness or social appropriateness. Now is not the time to be socially correct; now's the time to be spiritually urgent, which brings us to our next truth.

Third, every one of our children's destructive problems is a parent's urgent matter. These parents had come to the end of their efforts at securing help, healing, and deliverance for their children. In speaking of the importance of moving ahead on an important matter, in his famous "I Have a Dream" speech, Dr. Martin Luther King, Jr. said he had to "remind America of the fierce urgency of now." If the Negro was to be free, King said, "Now is the time."[1] If our children are to be free—healed, helped, and delivered—now is the time. Relief, release, and rescue cannot wait.

Fourth, the catalyst for healing and deliverance in the child is the faith of the parent. Critically ill, cripplingly dysfunctional, and cruelly deceived children cannot ask for themselves. Sometimes the obvious must be said. Children would rid themselves of the sickness, struggle, or satanic attack if they could. Not one of the children in the scenes above asked for help for themselves. The parents accepted the responsibility of getting help for them. Our faith must be firmly placed in the reality no problem of a child of God is hopeless. Our faith must move us on behalf of our children when a spirit blocks their hearing and ability to communicate (either physically, psychologically, or emotionally); when the problem is severe rebellion or cantankerousness; or when the problem is physical illness or involvement in a life-threatening activity or lifestyle. Our kids are dying and may not know it or realize the necessity of doing anything about it.

Now notice, I said "the catalyst for healing and deliverance in the child is the faith of the parent," not the result or the manifestation of the healing and deliverance. God is ultimately in control of all outcomes. As parents, we are no more to blame for the outcome of our adult children's poor decisions than we are to claim credit for their great ones. But the responsibility does lay in our laps to present the case to God.

Our children don't always consider that their decisions— bad or good—affect others in the community, church, and family. So, when they make a disquieting decision or behave unseemly, we ache for the fallout we know will follow, the pain they will inevitably face, and the situation into which everyone involved is now placed.

Finally, and central to the premise of this book, notice the child's age was not an issue when these biblical parents sought help for them. We're told Jairus's daughter was twelve, but we aren't told the age of the Canaanite woman's daughter. The father's demon-possessed son was a young adult, having been in his condition "since childhood," or literally "since he was a little boy."

So, where do we start at getting help for our children? First, start with a realization and a determination. Realize Jesus is the answer to our children's problems, no matter their issue and no matter their age. Armed with this realization, determine to take your child to Jesus. Second, believe. Have faith, Jesus can bring about the necessary change. Ignore the nay-sayers. Ignore the wind of culture and buck yourself up to walk directly into the gale. In addition to instantaneous healing, know help from God can come in many other forms including medication, counseling, a change of circumstances, etc. Whatever the God-honoring method of healing heaven sends our way, we must maintain our faith in the ability of Jesus to bring about revolutionary transformation.

How will we know God has moved in our children's lives? The mute will speak, the deaf will hear, the possessed will be sane, and the dead and dying will live again. The healing and deliverance of our children, no matter their age, lies in God's power to call "those things which do not exist as though they did," in Christ's power to be the embodiment of the healing word, and in the Holy Spirit's power to bring life to his truth (Romans 4:17). Our faith in the Trinity's ability is like our turning on the faucet to let the power flow into our children's lives.

Someone rightly said we need to stop telling God how big our problems are and start telling our problems how big our God is. Be encouraged. God loves our kids even more than we do. Believe like Jairus and take Jesus to your house. Believe like the Canaanite woman and insist upon even the crumbs. Believe like the young man's father and cry out to God to turn your belief into confident trust in Christ's ability to bring about the necessary changes. Join me, and the rest of the parents represented in this book, in our spiritual caravan. We're taking our children—with their adult problems—to Jesus, and we won't stop until they are healed.

—CHAPTER 2—
I'M PREGNANT OR MY GIRLFRIEND IS PREGNANT

THE SIMILAR CHRONICLES: YOU ARE NOT ALONE

DORINDA'S STORY

Both our daughters were intelligent and obedient; we never had any trouble out of them at all. They were A students, popular, and involved in school activities. More importantly, they were an integral part of the youth group at church—attending Sunday school, singing in the choir, and gladly participating in youth camps, plays, trips, and workshops. Their lives were full, and they were content in our home. They were good girls, and we were a happy little family—the first family of our church. My husband, their father, was the senior pastor.

About halfway through our older daughter's college career, she made a phone call which rocked my world. She was pregnant. Alison had planned to be a marine biologist, but now those plans were put on hold indefinitely. She returned home and returned to church. I handled the looks of derision from the congregants as best I could, while my husband bravely faced the turn of events head on. He told the congregation our children were no different from any other children, and children sometimes do things that disappoint us. We now had the opportunity to show love in the face of a family crisis. By exposing the skeleton, he showed shame only has the muscle we give it. Alison's beautiful baby, our first grandchild, became a light in our lives.

Five years later, our seventeen-year-old daughter called with a shaky voice. Her boyfriend, Louis (who we liked very much), had been visiting for the day. He wasn't driving his car, so she had left just forty-five minutes earlier to take him home. When I heard her voice on the phone, I thought maybe something went wrong with the car. If only it had been that simple.

Through tears, Joy said she had to tell me something. Then came the bombshell, and my world crashed to a halt. She was three months pregnant. She and Louis had kept the pregnancy a secret for a while, but now, after an argument, he threatened to break off the relationship. She counter-threatened to reveal their secret, and he dared her to do so. She made the call.

I told her, "Just come home. Calm down so you can be careful while you drive. We'll talk this over when you get here. "As I hung up the phone, I thought, *Oh no, not again! We'll be the laughingstock of the church for sure. My husband's a good man and a great pastor. The people will never respect him now. We can't go through this again.*

Honorably, Louis refused to let Joy face the music alone, so he returned with her. I hadn't told her father, so when they arrived, I told them to reveal the news to him together. They went downstairs into his office and told him. First, he paced, praying I'm sure, and then he told them, "You two have to decide what you're going to do." Then he sent them upstairs to the living room to talk it over.

I would not let this shame happen to our family again. Joy and Louis thought they were in love, and they'd get married. What did they know at seventeen? They hadn't even finished high school. This baby could never make an appearance.

The next day, I personally took Joy to a women's health clinic. They examined her and told us the results of the at-home pregnancy test had been a false positive. She had been missing her period because her fallopian tubes were dangerously blocked. She could die without corrective surgery as soon as possible. Fright and panic immediately replaced my shame. I drove Joy to the clinic the next morning. By three the same afternoon, she was home and on her menstrual cycle. But oddly enough, the clinic sent her home with only five, tiny red pills in a small, unmarked manila envelope and poorly typed instructions for personal care for the next three days.

The church never knew, but the truth became obvious when I drove past the women's "clinic" later—only to see pro-life picketers staked out in front. The workers inside dressed in nurses' garb were pro-choice devotees who had lied to us. The abortion haunted our family for years. Joy experienced years of grief, our relationship was strained, and she and Louis broke up.

I had been so ashamed of having two daughters get pregnant before marriage I allowed my embarrassment to completely eclipse the fact a beautiful child would be added to our family. Abortion looked like it was the right answer for all involved. My husband would not be looked down upon by the congregation, he and I would not be dishonored as bad parents, and my daughter could continue with her education and young adult life without the worries of raising a child. But once I allowed the truth to penetrate through these "rational excuses," the guilt of allowing the "clinic" to murder my innocent grandbaby came too late.

GRANT'S STORY

My twenty-year-old son, Diondre, was in his sophomore year at a prestigious university on a full football scholarship. He was so close to being on his way to the NFL, we could both taste it. I had nurtured his talent, especially after he came to live with me full time when his mom and I divorced. This boy was not only going to make it to a professional team, but he was also on track to be the greatest wide receiver the National Football League had ever seen.

Then came his announcement. He was home for Father's Day and said, "Dad, would you be proud of me no matter what I told you?" I knew something big was coming. I thought maybe he was doing bad in a class or had spent all his money.

"Dad, Regina is pregnant. The only way she'll be able to make it with a baby is if I quit school and get a job."

My first thought was to smack him in the head. I had warned him about women wanting a piece of him. My next thought was to scream, *Oh no, you don't. You are halfway there, and then the NFL draft. You're poised to go as an early pick. This ruins everything.*

As I looked at Diondre, I saw a man—a man ready to step up to his responsibilities. He was right—the only way he and Regina could support a baby was for someone to be working. That someone was him, the baby's daddy. He'll most likely never make the money an NFL career would have brought him, but he's starting out right in the lifelong career as a father. He's launching into an entry-level position at Regina's dad's company and is determined to still get his bachelor's degree in business by finishing school part time. He and Regina married three months before the arrival of my grandson. The little guy is built like a wide receiver.

THE STRESSFUL COMPLICATION: THE ISSUE

How do you handle your single daughter's shocking pregnancy announcement, or your son's surprising proclamation his girlfriend is carrying his child? It's tough to be calm when we know how much changes once one becomes a parent. We think about the obvious realities and difficulties our adult child will face, but we know the spiritual realities as well. This young person knows what the Scriptures say about premarital sex yet disobeyed those directives.

Now, here we are, looking at and listening to our baby who is about to have a baby. All we can think is, *she's not ready to nurture a baby,* or *he's not prepared to be someone's father*, or *they're babies themselves, how will they ever manage?*

The truth of the matter is this: many of us weren't ready to be parents either. We may have thought we were, but even when the couple is married, statistics show at least four in ten pregnancies in every state were unwanted or mistimed, according to the first-ever state-level analysis of unintended pregnancies.[1] Unreadiness is the least of our worries because deeper issues exist.

The premarital pregnancies of our children are such heart-rending issues for us Christian parents because, first and foremost, the world sees our kids are sexually active. Years ago, an unmarried, pregnant girl would have been considered "spoiled," and the young man would go unrevealed rather than be shown as the "spoiler." Parents would send the girls away to have the baby.

Although not the norm anymore, we are still bothered when our unmarried young adults are expecting a child. Our perturbation isn't making headway in the face of our current changing times. In 2009, the percentage of births to unmarried American women was 41.0 percent.[2] So with forty-one out of every one hundred babies being born out of wedlock, the traditional belief of premarital sex as a sin no longer has a measurable effect on behavior. Drawing the obvious from the above statistic, it follows many people regard marriage—the God-designed institution into which he intends children to be born—as an unnecessary distraction when deciding whether to bring a new life into the world.

I am not suggesting we throw up our hands and just float out with the tide, nor am I suggesting we go back to the days of sending girls "down south to live with Aunt Mae for a while." As believers in the truth of God's standards, we can't just shrug our shoulders as if everything is hunky-dory. When a premarital pregnancy happens, we need a message B—one starting by gently but firmly stating the facts of the situation. Although God is not surprised by this development, he's not pleased with it either. All babies are blessings, and God's not finished using the mother or the father in his kingdom. But we cannot gloss over the sin. God's grace and forgiveness do not give us a license to hold a different opinion than God holds regarding our transgressions.

Here's the hard part. We may unwittingly play a part in our children's nonchalant attitudes toward premarital sex. Perhaps discovering our unmarried adult children are sexually active is no longer a big deal to us. The low morals of society cause even Christian parents to assume our kids are intimately involved with their boyfriends or girlfriends. This laissez-faire attitude could be playing into the choices our young adults make.

We need to maintain a delicate balance. Let's consider the messages and attitudes of our conversations with our children. If we were celibate until marriage, do we hold it over our kids' heads as a live-up-to-what-I-did kind of message? Or if we weren't celibate before we got married, rather than being honest about the cost of the mistakes we made in our twenties, do we turn a blind, guilty eye, thinking we can't really say anything?

I was sick for several days after eating some chicken that had languished in the refrigerator a little too long. Since it was a stupid mistake, would I then ignore my child doing the same thing? Of course not. Based on the stupid choice we made of engaging in unmarried sex, why do we think we can't warn our kids of its drawbacks?

I know whereof I speak. At seventeen and unmarried, I ended an unwanted pregnancy with an abortion. That act wreaked havoc on my life and my ex-boyfriend's life for years. Later when I got married and had kids, I didn't want my boys to face the same pain. So, as each one reached the age of sixteen or seventeen, I told them the whole story—reasons, sin, rationalization, disappointment, disillusionment, divisiveness, long-term effects—everything. They didn't look down on me for the truth. To the contrary, they felt compassion for me. They understood I really understood what they faced in terms of sexual tension. They also understood my warnings were not just "Mom talking." I'd run into the fire and been burned. The emotional scars were third degree, and healing had been long and agonizing.

Additionally, maybe we're sending mixed messages because we don't truly believe our young adults can have the fortitude and Christian character to remain sexually pure until marriage. Why don't we believe God's word? God wouldn't tell us to "flee youthful lusts" and "abstain from fornication" if it were impossible for us to do so. Just as we gave them "the talk" when they were in middle and high school, we ought to keep giving them encouragement toward abstinence in their twenties.

There also exists a maddening double standard between how we address young adult women and young adult men. Somehow, we expect our daughters to hold out, but wink at the wild oat sowing of our sons. With whom do we think those sons are sowing those wild oats? With our daughters.

Relaxed societal morals, the double standard, and our message that young adults should delay sexual contact and marriage longer and longer, all set them up for sexual failure. These young people are in their sexual prime and are out from under our direct control for the first time during their late teens and early twenties. Then we're so devastated when pregnancies occur we're literally driving them to abortion clinics.

It's time to rethink the conversations we have with our kids about sex. First, we must believe the Bible's message about sexual activity. Second, we must engage them in intelligent conversation about the necessity for a clear line between society's morals about sexual activity and what we as Christians believe and why we believe it. Third, we need to eradicate the double standard. Finally, we may need to rethink our message about delaying marriage for so long.

THE SAVIOR'S COMMUNICATION:
THE BIBLE'S MESSAGE

The Bible teaches sexual intercourse is to be reserved for marriage. To understand the Bible's message, allow a few key passages to speak for themselves.

> Then the rib which the LORD God had taken from man He made into a woman, and He brought her to the man. And Adam said: "This *is* now bone of my bones
> And flesh of my flesh;
> She shall be called Woman,
> Because she was taken out of Man."
> Therefore a man shall leave his father and mother and be joined to his wife, and they shall become one flesh. (Genesis 2:22–24)
> Foods for the stomach and the stomach for foods, but God will destroy both it and them. Now the body *is* not for sexual immorality but for the Lord, and the Lord

for the body. And God both raised up the Lord and will also raise us up by His power. Do you not know that your bodies are members of Christ? Shall I then take the members of Christ and make *them* members of a harlot? Certainly not! Or do you not know that he who is joined to a harlot is one body *with her?* For "the two," He says, "shall become one flesh." But he who is joined to the Lord is one spirit *with Him.* Flee sexual immorality. Every sin that a man does is outside the body, but he who commits sexual immorality sins against his own body. Or do you not know that your body is the temple of the Holy Spirit *who is* in you, whom you have from God, and you are not your own? For you were bought at a price; therefore glorify God in your body and in your spirit, which are God's. (1 Corinthians 6:13–20)

Nevertheless, because of sexual immorality, let each man have his own wife, and let each woman have her own husband. Let the husband render to his wife the affection due her, and likewise also the wife to her husband. The wife does not have authority over her own body, but the husband *does.* And likewise the husband does not have authority over his own body, but the wife *does.* Do not deprive one another except with consent for a time, that you may give yourselves to fasting and prayer; and come together again so that Satan does not tempt you because of your lack of self-control. (1 Corinthians 7:2–5)

For this is the will of God, your sanctification: that you should abstain from sexual immorality; that each of you should know how to possess his own vessel in sanctification and honor, not in passion of lust, like the Gentiles who do not know God; that no one should take advantage of and defraud his brother in this matter, because the Lord *is* the avenger of all such, as we also forewarned you and testified. For God did not call us to uncleanness, but in holiness. (1 Thessalonians 4:3–7)

The four passages listed above are a representative sampling of the Bible's wisdom about premarital sex.

Intercourse is reserved to be practiced between a husband and wife (Genesis 2). Each person's human body is precious and has been created to be united with the Lord (1 Corinthians 6). Immorality disrupts our fellowship with the Lord. Why? Because the basis of immorality is self-governance and self-gratification—doing what we want to do to, rather than what God wants us to do, to bring ourselves fulfillment and pleasure. To avoid the minefield of immorality, God has instituted marriage as the safe and approved relationship in which sexual intercourse—the physical picture of our spiritual union with God—can take place (1 Corinthians 7). God has called us to live holy lives in our singleness, and one huge aspect of this holiness is abstinence (1 Thessalonians 4).

DRAW A CLEAR LINE

The important thing to remember is neither God's truth nor God's love ever changes. To stand true to Scripture regarding this issue, as with all the issues we cover in this book, it's important to draw a clear line between what the Bible says and what culture says. Because of society's relaxed moral standards concerning premarital sex, and although it will probably be tempting to avoid uncomfortable conversations which identify the practice as wrong, we must lovingly hold to God's truth.

Let's be clear. This is the Bible's message and teaching it to our young people well in advance of the onset of puberty will go a long way in fortifying their personal resolve once they hit those teen and young adult years. Even when we have raised our children to understand the solid truth of Scripture about premarital sex, they will ultimately be individually responsible for their sexual purity.

When our young adult children choose to be sexually active before marriage, we must allow the outcome, consequences, and responsibilities to be their own. In other words, since our son is old enough to create a child, he should now take on the full responsibility of fathering the child and providing a covering for his child's mother. Since our daughter behaved as an adult by participating in sexual intercourse, she should now live with the full accountability of motherhood and understand the need to respect her baby's father. They want adult joys; they must take on adult jobs.

ERADICATE THE DOUBLE STANDARD

The Bible's message on sexual abstinence is equal opportunity. It doesn't discriminate on the basis of gender. None of the Bible's verses on the subject of fornication tell women to abstain but men to indulge. Both men and women are instructed to wait until marriage to have sexual intercourse.

It's not so much the direct message we as parents often send to young men is the problem. Our young men and women hear the exact same message in church from their pastors, but the subliminal messages of the culture (and even from parents sometimes) set a double standard. A young woman who has "given it up" to various boyfriends is thought to be a slut, but a young man who has had multiple conquests is winked at, patted on the back, and considered to be a stud. The girl who says no is looked upon by her contemporaries as stuck-up, arrogant (thinking she's too good for anyone), a prude, holier-than-thou, old-fashioned, or simply a bore. Eyebrows are raised—maybe she's a lesbian.

Still, fathers protect their daughters and warn them about men and boys who are "only after one thing," but they tell their sons to be sure to carry condoms to protect themselves from STDs and getting a girl pregnant. The son is not expected to even consider abstinence as an option. If he did, his father and his friends feel justified in accusing him of being gay.

Even the young men themselves reinforce the double standard. The young ladies who easily say yes to sex knock themselves out of the running as wife material. Guys do not want those girls to ultimately be the mother of their children. A Christian young man in his early twenties told me candidly, "No, I'd never even consider marrying the girls who chase me and say 'yes' to me immediately. Sure, I'll kick it with them, but they won't be my wife. I know some girls who like me, and I like them, but I've never had sex with them. I'm keeping them in my back pocket for when I'm ready to settle down."

The challenge is huge. We must encourage abstinence until marriage with both our sons and daughters. Young women must be empowered to say no until marriage and be encouraged in their stand not only by adults, but also by their friends who hold the same standards. Young men must be challenged to accept sexual purity as a badge of honor, as the highest gift they can give their future wife who will be their life companion. For both sexes, controlling their sexual passions before marriage will translate into dedication to God and to the commitment which they make to each other during marriage.

With the previous thoughts in mind, perhaps it's time to rethink the messages we're giving to our young adults about how long they should wait before considering marriage. Economic issues are important, but such concerns must be tempered by our spiritual understanding. Marriage is a good thing and can be so for young people in their twenties. The first thing ever recorded as not good was man being alone. God had a remedy. He turned bad into good by giving the first man a wife (See Genesis 2:18–24). The New Testament explains marriage not only supplies good companionship but is a picture of the relationship between Christ and the Church (See Ephesians 5:22–33).

One element of the glue holding decades-long marriages together is making it through those early years without a lot of creature comforts. Getting through hard times together is not the only link. Building something from next-to-nothing together is one of the factors strengthening the marriage bond. Perhaps if our young adults were encouraged to marry earlier rather than later, much of the sexual promiscuity among our Christian young people could be averted. So, what if it might be hard work for young couples to have to work together to meet their financial obligations? Most couples must do that anyway, regardless of their ages when they marry.

THE SINCERE CARE-FRONTATION

Empathetic listening tops the charts as a vital skill to be employed when faced with the unplanned pregnancy involving our sons and daughters. They approach us steeling themselves against the unknown about how we'll react to the news. How do you care for and confront your sexually active young adult daughter or son? Our most important obligation to our children, regardless of age, is to communicate genuine concern for them and for our relationship with them. When informed about the unplanned pregnancy, we'd be wise to take a calming breath and turn our concern to them and away from ourselves. This pregnancy is neither about our reputation nor us—it's about the expectant parents and the precious unborn child. Our desire for a harmonious relationship with our child will be apparent as we remain calm and open in the following areas.

OPEN ARMS

Children don't want to disappoint us, or worse yet, lose our love. Our daughter or son has suffered under the weight of apprehension about our reaction ever since she or he learned about the pregnancy. Let her reveal the truth; let him tell you the news. Then without a word, wrap your arms around your child and hold on as long as necessary to let the child know not even this can snatch your love away.

This one act will probably open the floodgates for you both, and it will accomplish two things. First, your child will be comforted. There's no better feeling than relief from dread. Also, the inborn longing for the safety and shelter of Daddy and Mommy never really goes away, so this hug reaffirms your love as an unalterable haven. Second, this embrace will give you a much-needed moment to collect your thoughts. Silently fling your immediate thoughts of your personal hurt or embarrassment or disappointment into the Lord's lap and ask him to act through you for what your child, and your developing grandchild, need right now.

OPEN EARS

Once the initial embrace ends, sit back and listen. Pamela and Elvin found her father's calm response surprising yet immediately comforting and empowering when together, they approached him with the news of Pamela's unplanned pregnancy. Her father, Mr. Isaac, listened as Pamela broke the news, and then Elvin took the conversation from there. Her father's loving silence allowed Elvin to rise to the occasion and man-up to his responsibilities. Elvin apologized to Mr. Isaac for running ahead of the proper order, which should have been marriage first. Elvin wanted Mr. Isaac to know he loved his daughter and had every intention of caring for both her and their child.

Granted, not every story will end as well as Pamela and Elvin's did, but every young person facing an unplanned pregnancy needs the listening ear of the parent(s) to whom they turn. Let your daughter pour out her heart about how she's feeling emotionally, physically, and spiritually. Let your son express his fears. Remember, they are about to give birth to your legacy—your grandchild.

OPEN HEART

As your daughter talks, listen. Listen not with the idea of what you are going to say next. Listen empathetically to what she says. Sympathy means you feel the sorrow of the other person as the current situation is faced. Empathy means you vicariously take the sorrow on as your own. In other words, you can put yourself into your daughter's shoes. As she talks, become her, pregnant at her age, and in her present situation.

- I'm still in school. Will I be able to graduate? My job only pays X-amount.
- How will I support a baby?
- I'm living in the dorm. Where will I live with a baby?
- Should I marry the baby's father? Do I love him?
- Oh, my goodness; I'm going to be somebody's mother!

As your son is talking, become him in his present situation at his age with his girlfriend pregnant.

- I never intended for my girlfriend to get pregnant. What am I supposed to do now?
- I had plans. How will my plans be affected?
- Is my life over?
- Am I supposed to marry my baby's mother? Do I even love her? I don't even know a lot about her.
- How can I make enough money to support a baby when I can barely support myself?
- Oh, my goodness; I'm going to be somebody's father!

Our turn to speak comes after our child has finished revealing the situation. Start by communicating back to her all she has said, letting her know you have indeed heard her heart. Echo back to your son what he has told you so you both clearly see you understand. Then start communicating facts from your more mature perspective.

First, encourage the continuation of the pregnancy. Abortion is not an option as the horrendous outcome is always the death of an innocent child.

Second, calmly communicate the truth about the responsibilities of parenthood. Let the new parents know your love and support does not mean you will become the parent of your grandchild. Your daughter is the mother, or your son is the father. All the parenting responsibilities are theirs. As one father said to his son in that situation, ask "So what are you going to do?" Talk through the immediate options.

1. Prenatal care and parenting classes
2. Marriage
3. Adoption
4. Joint custody if marriage is not chosen
5. Living arrangements
6. Childcare
7. Employment options and choices

THE SWEET COMMUNION: HOW TO PRAY

Start by remembering "children are a gift of the LORD, the fruit of the womb is a reward" (Psalm 127:3 NLT). Sometimes it's easy to forget when our children become young adults, and we feel the pangs of their actions. Matthew Henry's commentary of Psalm 127 poignantly ends with this statement.

> Observe here, *Children of the youth* are *arrows in the hand*, which, with prudence, may be directed aright to the mark, God's glory and the service of their generation; but afterwards, when they have gone abroad into the world, they are arrows out of the hand; it is too late to bend them then. But these arrows in the hand too often prove arrows in the heart, a constant grief to their godly parents, whose gray hairs they bring with sorrow to the grave.[3]

Regardless of what our children do, they are our gifts from the Lord, and they don't stop being so when their behavior disappoints us. Remember, thankfully, we don't stop belonging to God when we do what he doesn't like.

So, start with a prayer of adoration to God, acknowledging in his ears who you know him to be. Then confess personal shortcomings and sins. Next, ask God for your heart's desires. Close by thanking him. Your prayer may be something like this:

God, you are awesome in your ideas about the family. Children were and are your wonderful idea. You are the giver and sustainer of the life of my children and the life of the growing child in my daughter's (or my son's girlfriend's) womb. You are the heavenly Father of my child and my grandchild. Bless your holy name.

Now God, I confess my sin of ... (Perhaps here you need to discard your anger, confess your self-centered thoughts of your own reputation, or admit the hatred you feel toward your daughter's boyfriend or your son's girlfriend. Whatever your shortcomings are related to this unplanned pregnancy, pour them out here to Jesus. Even take time here to allow him to point out some out you may not have yet identified and still need to confess.)

Next, *God, I ask you to help my child make the right decisions regarding this unborn child. This baby is a surprise to us, but not to you. Please provide all the necessary love, money, and other resources to support the life of this child. May this child be whole, healthy, and a blessing to the world.*

Finally, God, thank you for being our guide as we journey through this situation. Thank you for the knowledge you will never leave or forsake us. Surround us with your wisdom and peace. Even in this, let us be a witness to the world of your love, mercy, and grace.

In Jesus's strong name, Amen.

THE SUPPORTIVE CONNECTIONS:
WHERE TO TURN FOR ADDITIONAL HELP

- Option Line—http://www.optionline.org/abortioneducation. This website is an easy-to-use site that quickly answers questions about pregnancy and abortion.

- National Right to Life League—https://www.nrlc.org. The mission statement of the NRLL is: The mission of National Right to Life is to protect and defend the most fundamental right of humankind, the right to life of every innocent human being from the beginning of life to natural death. The national office contact information is: 512 10th Street NW, Washington, DC 20004, (202) 626-8800

- National Adoption Center—http://www.adopt.org/assembled/mission.html. The National Adoption Center expands adoption opportunities for children living in foster care throughout the United States and is a resource to families and to agencies who seek the permanency of caring homes for children.

—CHAPTER 3—
I'M GAY

THE SIMILAR CHRONICLES: YOU ARE NOT ALONE

MONIQUE'S STORY

We decided to call her Amanda. She was a beautiful girl with a smooth, caramel complexion. We watched her grow up with talents in the arts; however, her love for music was greater. Amanda, like most girls, played with other girls, laughed, and enjoyed the things and activities of young girls up until the summer prior to her freshmen year of college when she began to refuse the feminine look and the attentions of boys. As her parents, we talked with her about how we felt about the changes we were seeing in her preferences. It didn't matter to us she dressed in clothes she felt were comfortable for her, but we communicated we were concerned this transformation seemed to be extending into disassociating herself from the gender into which she was born. We also discussed the position of the Bible and the church regarding the lifestyle of same sex relationships. We prayed after those talks, yet we continued to observe more changes in her clothing. She avoided any activities labeled "feminine" and withdrew from any type of relationship with boys. No matter how many times we or other family members or friends asked, "Are you gay?" Amanda quickly responded, "No. I keep telling you no." Amanda appeared appalled at questions about her sexual orientation. Still, we noticed her smile and the sparkle in her eyes were gone.

Then, during one Christmas break, we got a call from Amanda as she was coming from the movies. She was upset and kept repeating, "I love her. I love her." The phone conversation was confusing and disconcerting. Her emotions were running high, so we couldn't clearly understand her. Finally, she stopped yelling and began to sob quietly as she explained why she was angry and upset. The family of her close female friend would not tolerate their daughter's relationship with Amanda and were willing to go to jail after a fight if necessary. When they had asked Amanda if she was gay and if something were going on between her and their daughter, all she could answer was, "I love her."

After this incident, Amanda's church attendance decreased, and she attended fewer family events and holidays, but she would not admit to a lesbian lifestyle. The distance and secrets worsened, as did Amanda's weight gain, self-care, and sadness. During the summer prior to her sophomore year, she planned a trip to visit a family member in Texas. We later discovered she was meeting someone in Florida with whom she had connected via the internet. The whole ordeal of her nonverbal acknowledgment of her lifestyle went to a new level. Her associates became more invisible to our household, and her joy seemed to disappear as well.

After we engaged in much prayer and fasting, Amanda returned home. She refused to go to professional counseling; however, she met with friends and clergy of our church for brief conversations about her lifestyle. She admitted to the pastor she was a lesbian, yet she still would not tell her family. Her admission finally became clear one Mother's Day when

Amanda attempted to encourage me by writing in the card, "Momma, you raised us right according to the Bible. I know what I am doing—it is my choice, which I know is wrong."

Her card gave me a sense of peace. God is the One who convinces and convicts as he turns the hearts of our loved ones. Her lesbian issue was not over, however. She then delivered news not matching her current lifestyle. She became pregnant and decided to keep the baby.

This new life as a mother no doubt caused her to look at womanhood in a new way as she vacillated over her choice of lesbianism. Our granddaughter is growing up and, at four-years-old, started requesting her mother take her to church and paint her nails. She tells her mother girls wear skirts. I truly believe the Lord is working through this child to draw her mother to his love.

This has been a journey of trying to understand many things. I have asked, "Why, God, is our daughter living like this?" "When will change come?" "Whose fault is this?"

"[God] sent His word to heal them and to deliver *them* from their destruction" (Psalm 107:20). Living with shame, disappointment, and guilt lessened when this Scripture became *rhema* in my heart—God's specific direction as to how I was to personally apply this Scripture to my life. The encouragement is God sent his word to heal and deliver anyone spiritually, emotionally, and physically if they accept and apply biblical truths.

We have learned we can extend unconditional love to our daughter without accepting her ungodly lifestyle. She knows the truth, as we have demonstrated Christian living in our home and have trained her in Christian principles. But the journey is not over. Although it should be getting easier with time, our Amanda has taken yet another turn in her lifestyle choice and has decided to start gender reassignment. Tears flow as I tell you her elementary-aged daughter is now asking me, "Why is Mommy trying to become a boy?"

We realize, as parents, we are not penalized for Amanda's adult choices, and although it's encouraging to pray and live a blessed life, this one is a really tough issue. I learned no matter whether we have a gay son, a lesbian daughter, a child choosing gender reassignment, or one who prefers any number of the other politically correct titles like queer, transgender, bisexual, questioning, intersexual, asexual, aromantic, pansexual, or kink—the blurring of the gender lines challenges our sensibilities, our understandings, and our faith.

THE STRESSFUL COMPLICATION: THE ISSUE

Let's face it: the issue in this chapter could be the reason many purchasers bought this book. As this book goes to print, the conversation about the right or wrong, acceptance or rejection, and the good or bad of homosexuality inundates the airwaves and our conversations. People from neither side seem willing to listen to or understand the other's arguments. I hope my presentation of the biblical perspective will at least be clear. If readers choose to be at odds with the following Scriptures, their disagreement is between them and the Author of the Book. With this issue, as well as with every other issue in life, the responses and opinions of believers in Christ must line up with God's word, not with feelings, social mores, peer pressure, learned habits, legislation, or personal connections.

In Nathaniel Hawthorne's haunting tale, "The Minister's Black Veil," the Puritan pastor, Rev. Hooper, showed up behind his pulpit one Sunday morning wearing a black veil obscuring most of his face. His parishioner's curiosity turned to uneasiness and even fear as weeks turned to months and then to years with the minister refusing to remove the disturbing covering. He wore it at funerals and at weddings alike. His congregants stopped inviting him to sit with them at church suppers. He lost his fiancée due to his refusal to remove it even for her. Hawthorne never reveals why Rev. Hooper began to wear the veil, but at length, it came to stand as the symbol of the secret sin resident in every human heart.[1]

Hawthorne's gripping tale comes to mind in a particularly forceful manner as we grapple with the issue of homosexuality. Just as Rev. Hooper's black veil caused his congregants to question the presence of some sin and guilt in his life, so, too, does the admission of same sex attraction cause us to point the finger of condemnation at the one who makes such a revelation. However, at the outset of our present discussion, let's not forget Rev. Hooper's veil enlightened him to the grim reality that "behold, on *every* visage, a black veil."[2]

Few of the subjects covered in this book will elicit as strong a response as does this homosexuality issue. Parents are concerned to discover their children are pregnant out of wedlock, involved with drugs, quitting school, or in trouble with the law; but concern transforms into utter dismay, heartbreak, and even despair when they learn their kids are gay. The reaction mirrors the stages of grief—shock, denial, pain, anger, and depression. We are led to believe that only in rare cases, at the first revelation, do families experience an upward turn, reconstruction, and acceptance.

Here's the problem. If we're honest, most of us are more lenient to excuse—or at least tolerantly discuss and try to understand—habits and lifestyles in which we ourselves have participated. For example, reformed liars don't believe lying is right, but when confronting other liars, they understand why they lie and can gently direct them toward reform. Renewed adulterers know it was wrong to commit adultery, but when confronting other adulterers, they get how and why such situations evolve and can tenderly challenge the current wrongdoer.

But most of us have never walked in the shoes of someone who is physically attracted to others of the same sex, so we don't understand how a person can feel this attraction. Add to this the major difference of the mindset which believes, unlike with lying and adultery, homosexual activities are not wrong, and we have our present distress. Former cultural norms listed homosexual deeds among sinful lifestyles, but society is doing its best to change this view. Is participating in same-sex sexual exploits just like being a liar or an adulterer? If so, the liar, the adulterer, and the involved homosexual must all be treated the same. They, like all the rest of us, must receive with love the teaching of the truth which is to turn from each sinful action to obedience to God to bring him glory.

This issue is of particular concern to Christian parents because we have raised our children, prayed for them, and held certain assumptions and dreams for them. We figured they'd travel the school track—elementary, to high school, to college. We also assumed they would eventually be on the family track—out of our house, working a job, getting married, and having families of their own to give us grandchildren. We definitely prayed they would be on the faith track and continue to follow the Lord, so we'd all end up in heaven together. The announcement of homosexuality pops the balloon of the marriage and family assumption we held of our child uniting with a spouse of the opposite sex. Grave concerns about our child's place in heaven are likely to arise as well.

THE SAVIOR'S COMMUNICATION: THE BIBLE'S MESSAGE

As with every other issue we're touching on in this book, we want to approach this one biblically. What does the Bible say about homosexuality?

The rise of societal acceptance of the homosexual lifestyle can be traced to the early 1970s when homosexuality was removed from the American Psychological Association's (APA) handbook as a mental/physical diagnosis.[3] The change—coupled with greater activism seen in LGBTQ+ organizations, websites, blogs, the entertainment industry, and individuals in our current culture—tries to explain away the Bible's teaching on this subject, but the Bible is amazingly clear. As an introduction to the actual passages themselves, here's what Louis and Melissa McBurney had to say in *Christian Sex Rules: A Guide to What's Allowed in the Bedroom.*

> There are some specific sexual behaviors that are forbidden in Scriptures. Adultery, that is having sexual intercourse with another person's spouse or a partner other than your own spouse, is a sin. Jesus, in the Sermon on the Mount, deepens the importance of marital faithfulness by extending the prohibition of infidelity to include a lustful thought life as well as the physical act of intercourse.
> Looking into our minds and hearts is an important principle for safeguarding the delights of intimacy. The Bible also lists other practices that are "abominations" to God (Leviticus 18, Romans 1:21–32, 1 Thessalonians 4:1–8, and 1 Corinthians 6:12–20). These include homosexuality, bestiality, and incest.[4]

Be aware, the following Scriptures are labeled "clobber passages" by some gay people. They say straight, religious people quote these verses for the purpose of clobbering them over the head to make them feel bad about being gay. This defense is equivalent to hearing an adulterer, a liar, or a thief complain about being clobbered by any Scriptures that speak specifically against those sins. No, these Scriptures are not clobbering. Like all the rest of the words in the Bible, the Scriptures are declaring God's heart and intention.

When the adulterer hears, "Thou shalt not commit adultery," there's really no argument to be made. The Bible says what it says. When the thief reads, "Thou shalt not steal," those words cannot simply be cut out of the Bible and the reader pretend the hole in the page existed all along. And when the liar is exposed to the commandment teaching, "Thou shalt not bear false witness against thy neighbor," there's no legitimate excuse of being born a liar and so always living as a liar. No matter our natural inclinations, Scripture declares and requires we change our ways to meet the Bible's clear proclamations. It is not our prerogative to announce, "Well, this is my truth." Since we believe the Bible to contain the declared word of God, only its truth matters.

Let's examine Scriptures on homosexuality using this same criterion. For the sake of clarity, I list three Bible versions for each passage: the New King James Version, the New Living Translation, and The Message.

> Leviticus 18:22
>
> You shall not lie with a male as with a woman. It *is* an abomination.
>
> Do not practice homosexuality, having sex with another man as with a woman. It is a detestable sin. (NLT)
>
> Don't have sex with a man as one does with a woman. That is abhorrent. (MSG)

Romans 1:21–32. Please read the entire passage for the context. In summation, humankind made the decision to turn from God to what it made and wants for itself. Once the decision was made, verses 26–28 declare:

> For this reason, God gave them up to vile passions. For even their women exchanged the natural use for what is against nature. Likewise, also the men, leaving the natural use of the woman, burned in their lust for one

another, men with men committing what is shameful, and receiving in themselves the penalty of their error which was due. And even as they did not like to retain God in *their* knowledge, God gave them over to a debased mind, to do those things which are not fitting.

That is why God abandoned them to their shameful desires. Even the women turned against the natural way to have sex and instead indulged in sex with each other. And the men, instead of having normal sexual relations with women, burned with lust for each other. Men did shameful things with other men, and as a result of this sin, they suffered within themselves the penalty they deserved. Since they thought it foolish to acknowledge God, he abandoned them to their foolish thinking and let them do things that should never be done. (NLT)

Worse followed. Refusing to know God, they soon didn't know how to be human either—women didn't know how to be women, men didn't know how to be men. Sexually confused, they abused and defiled one another, women with women, men with men—all lust, no love. And then they paid for it, oh, how they paid for it—emptied of God and love, godless and loveless wretches. Since they didn't bother to acknowledge God, God quit bothering them and let them run loose. (MSG)

1 Corinthians 6:9–10

Do you not know that the unrighteous will not inherit the kingdom of God? Do not be deceived. Neither fornicators, nor idolaters, nor adulterers, nor homosexuals, nor sodomites, nor thieves, nor covetous, nor drunkards, nor revilers, nor extortioners will inherit the kingdom of God.

Don't you realize that those who do wrong will not inherit the Kingdom of God? Don't fool yourselves. Those who indulge in sexual sin, or who worship idols, or commit adultery, or are male prostitutes, or practice homosexuality, or are thieves, or greedy people, or drunkards, or are abusive, or cheat people—none of these will inherit the Kingdom of God. (NLT)

> Don't you realize that this is not the way to live? Unjust
> people who don't care about God will not be joining in
> his kingdom. Those who use and abuse each other, use
> and abuse sex, use and abuse the earth and everything
> in it, don't qualify as citizens in God's kingdom. (MSG)

After reading these passages of Scripture (one from the Old Testament, two from the New), the Bible's position should be clear—practices associated with homosexuality are sin. But you will find many people who identify themselves as Bible-believing Christians disagreeing with these Scriptures. *How*, they ask, *can the way people are born label them as abominable sinners?* Let's explore this question with an illustration.

I knew a little boy who was a thief. Having known this child from his birth, I witnessed how he continually acted out his predisposition. I would have to shake him down whenever he was ready to leave my home at the end of a play date because he'd always be hiding one of my son's toys. No one taught this child to steal. Stealing was a part of him—an inborn, "natural" reaction.

What were adults supposed to do about this boy's habit of stealing? Were we expected to notice his predisposition to pilfering, pat him on the back in congratulations, and raise him to be the best possible larcenist he could grow up to be? Of course not. Our responsibility was to point out the error of his ways and teach him how to live in opposition to his "natural" tendencies. Why? Because his "natural" tendencies were leading him to wrong actions—actions the Bible labeled as sin. Did we hate the child? No. Were we judging him? No. We were pointing out to him what he needed to know to live for God as he should, even though living as he should went against his "natural" feelings.

According to *The Independent*, July 2, 2015, a publication out of the United Kingdom, there was a scientific study of 409 pairs of gay brothers. The study made the following points:

Research conducted by the NorthShore Research Institute in the US found clear links between male sexual orientation and two specific regions of the human genome, with the lead scientist Alan Sanders declaring that the work "erodes the notion that sexual orientation is a choice." The study is three times larger than any previously done and highlights two genetic regions that have been tied to male homosexuality in separate research: Xq28, first identified in 1993, and 8q12, spotted in 2005.

However, Sanders does not claim to have identified a single gene which 'causes' male homosexuality in humans and stresses that with complex human traits like sexual orientation there are many influencing factors, both genetic and environmental.

When asked, "How big is the role genetics play in sexual orientation?" Dr. Alan Sanders himself answered:
It's not as high as a lot of conditions that are studied genetically. It is low to moderate heritability. There are different estimates. Maybe somewhere around thirty to forty percent of the variation ... When people say there is the "gay gene" it's an oversimplification. We don't think there is just one gene involved. There are a number of genes. We also don't think genetics is the whole story. It's not.[5]

Even though this study found "two genetic regions that have been tied to male homosexuality in separate research," notice Sanders does not claim to have identified a single gene which "causes" male homosexuality in humans.

Regardless of studies, whether our predispositions are tied to genetics does not matter in the spiritual scheme of things. God has said we are in sin if we think on and then carry out lying, stealing, promiscuity, or homosexuality.

Thanks to our original parents, we are *all* born with a sin nature separating us from God. We are *all* hopeless, wretched, abominable sinners who are *all* called upon by Scripture to turn from our natural, sinful tendencies, surrendering them and presenting our very bodies as living sacrifices. (See Romans 12:1–2).

The temptation to lie is not the problem. Telling the lie and identifying oneself as a liar is the sin. Almost sneaking the item from the store is not the problem. Stealing the item is the sin. A guy desiring to have sex with his girlfriend is not the problem. Performing the sex act with her is the sin. Feeling attracted to the same sex is not the problem. Carrying out that attraction as one would sexually with the opposite sex is the sin. Once I realize I have a tendency of being what God said I should not be—a liar, a thief, promiscuous, gay, or anything else—I need to surrender the tendency to God to allow him to help me live within his word instead. The tendency in question may be part of my family history and my DNA make-up, but if acting on it dishonors God, with the power of the Holy Spirit, I get to glorify God as I defy it.

The battle is being waged over these passages of Scripture—Leviticus 18:22, Romans 1:21–32, and 1 Corinthians 6:9–10. Organizations started by and composed of LGBTQ+* individuals and allies state their purpose as reaching into traditional churches to get them to understand and accept members of their community. The aim of these organizations is to publish books, conduct seminars, and involve themselves in activities to change the understanding of these passages and thereby, change society's view—and especially the church's view—of homosexuality. (*LGBTQ stands for lesbian, gay, bisexual, transgender, questioning/queer, and more.[6])

Let's be completely clear: The liar is not to be hated. The adulterer is not to be hated. The thief is not to be hated. The homosexual is not to be hated. Pointing out what the Bible says about the actions of people in each of the above categories is not hate, it is reporting what the Bible says about those actions. God loves the people and so should we. God's love is the very reason why he's taken the time to point out his best for all of us and where we go wrong.

The most problematic issue arises with the attempt to change the understanding of Scripture. *How*, we question, *can young people who were raised in church now be incorporating a belief about homosexuality which is so far removed from the original understanding of the Scriptures?* The answer is as close as the first book of the Bible.

Genesis chapter three relates the occurrence of the fall of man. We hear the satanically possessed, cunning serpent pose to Eve the Bible's first question, "Has God indeed said, 'You shall not eat of every tree of the garden?'" (v.1). This one query set into motion the series of events leading to the original sin, which got all our problems started.

God had told his first humans they could eat from every tree of the garden except the Tree of Knowledge of Good and Evil. Don't miss that—they *could eat* from *every tree* except one. Satan flipped the script and misquoted God. He twisted the question and asked, "Didn't God say you *couldn't eat* from *every* tree?" God's words had emphasized how he had abundantly supplied. Satan's words twisted God's intent by emphasizing the one thing God was keeping from them.

Satan, the enemy of our souls, continues to play the same word games today to spin our understanding away from having a godly viewpoint. God's word clearly outlines the fact one man is to marry one woman, engage in intimate sexual relations for each other's pleasure, and have children to raise up a godly heritage. Marriage is good, sex is good, having children is good, but Satan twists this plan by suggesting same-sex couples should be able to enjoy the same God-ordained privileges heterosexual couples enjoy. Believing Satan's twists became our tumble.

THE SINCERE CARE-FRONTATION

So how do you care for and confront your same sex attracted (SSA) young adult daughter or son?

Establish Love Still Exists

First, establish the fact you love your child. Remember love is not proven by acceptance of everything the loved one does or believes. Many times, love is proven by restrictions placed to keep the loved one from hurt, harm, and danger.

Explain Your Stand on the Word

Second, possibly using the above illustration of the boy born a liar as an explanation, recognize and clearly establish that homosexuality is what the Bible says it is.

Extend Your Willingness to Understand

One of the surest ways to communicate our willingness to get to know others is to learn to speak their language, so the third way to engage in care-frontation is to speak the language of your child identifying as a homosexual. Being able to speak the language will open two opportunities: A–to clearly hear what's being said, and B–to clearly communicate your points. Know basic definitions so what you mean to communicate is not confused by words that have been redefined.

After several years of back-and-forth conversations with her son who classified himself as gay, one Christian mother felt it was time to write a prayed over and well-crafted letter to her son explaining in writing her biblical position regarding his lifestyle. In the letter, she laid out Scriptures and an explanation of what she wanted him to understand. He sent back two responses to which she also had ready answers.

Her son's first response was, "You don't seem to accept I'm gay," to which she answered, "Just to be clear, I 'accept' you are gay in the same way I 'accept' any other obvious situation I see, good or bad. But all realities cannot be celebrated."

Next, her son related, "What I pray for you to do is open up your heart to things which may seem to be going against what you think."

This comment brought a longer, more precise clarification. The mother responded, "This is not about what I think. It's totally about what I know to be biblically true. As hard and uncomfortable as it feels, we must adjust our lives to fit the Word, not the other way around."

ENDURE WITH CALMNESS AND CONSISTENCY

Affirming our love, establishing our biblical position, and doing our best to speak the language should communicate our strong desire to work together to maintain a harmonious relationship. With that in mind, the fourth way we show care-frontation is by remaining calm yet consistent.

EXPRESS LOVE AND PRIDE ABOUT OTHER ASPECTS OF YOUR CHILD'S LIFE

Our sons and daughters who identify as gay have many gifts and talents to be complimented and applauded. We can continue to express our pride in their accomplishments and our appreciation of them as great human beings. We can celebrate the attributes of our children who are smart, resourceful, kind, sensitive, witty, thoughtful, and good citizens, among hundreds of other positive character traits they possess.

ENCOURAGE AND AFFIRM INNOCENT SAME-SEX FRIENDSHIPS

There absolutely is a place in our lives for same-sex relationships—they are called friendships. Same-sex friendships are vital and healthy as long as they stop short of sexual involvement. The innocent same-sex friendships enjoyed by children in the fifties and sixties now risk the possibility of being slanderously accused of having gay overtones. Of course, not all same-sex friendships succumb, but Satan is making sure the constant barrage of messages pushing the acceptance of SSA relationships is placing a huge temptation on same-sex friendships to move to a sexual level.

Just the suggestion is a toehold for the friends to begin considering whether they are homosexuals. Throw in a conflict with a friend of the opposite sex, and a toehold can quickly become a foothold encouraging further investigation. If an investigation takes place, the friends can then find themselves in a stronghold moving deeper and deeper into gay identification through new acquaintances and society's continued push toward the acceptance of the lifestyle as normal. Soon most of life's decisions become governed by sexual identity—where to live, where to work, where to attend church, what to wear, how to act, who to befriend, etc. The stronghold transforms into a stranglehold—just what Satan wanted. The enemy has successfully stolen, killed, and destroyed this child's original God-given birth identity. Deliverance on the spiritual level is then the only answer for extraction from the acceptance of an identity God's word clearly shows he never intended.

A SPECIAL COMMUNICATION

One of my acquaintances, Lori Wildenberg, sent me a very special account concerning our current conversation. Her daughter not only consented for her to share these words, but she influenced some of the thoughts in this book. I thought it timely and poignant. Here it is.

> My twenty-seven-year-old daughter has been mistaken for a man. She has short, jet-black hair and sometimes sports a shaved head. She wears

guys' clothes. Her gestures and the way she carries herself convey a masculine message. When she hears someone say, "Excuse me, sir," she shrugs it off. I, on the other hand, feel like I've just taken a sucker punch to the gut.

The news about celebrity transgender individuals hits a little too close to home. Some camps celebrate and call these transgendered persons "heroes." Other groups turn their noses up in disgust.

We, as a society, have missed the mark on how to respond to these troubled souls. Since I have a young adult who struggles with gender identification issues, here are some questions I have pondered:

- Why are we so intolerant of the effeminate male and the masculine female?
- Isn't there room for a man with a gentle soul?
- Can't we make space for a powerful woman?
- Can't a man operate out of his feelings?
- Isn't it okay if a woman is a thinker rather than a feeler?
- Why is there such a narrow stereotype of what constitutes a man or a woman?

We have created a very small box for the two genders. Now for clarification, I am not talking about the current philosophy of the gender spectrum. Men are men if they are XY and women are women if they are XX. Chromosomes determine sex not behaviors or preferences. I am also not addressing jobs or roles, only personality and interests. Two people who have busted the glass ceiling of stereotypes are Mikhail Baryshnikov, the amazing dancer who is a man, and Laila Ali, the amazing boxer who is a woman.

I don't have any answers, but I do know how to respond to the person who is outside the box. I must respond with love and compassion. Here are a few things I have learned.

1. We affirm how God created the person (male or female); for instance, "God created you to be a gentle man. Being gentle is a strength." Or "God created you to be a strong, assertive woman. Strength and assertion are strengths."

2. We don't enter into our children's delusions or illusions of being another sex by calling them by a different name or referring to them as the opposite sex (Genesis 1:27).

3. We pray for their relationship with the Lord.

My daughter suggested I google the name "Sy Rogers." Sy wrestled with his gender identity since he was a young boy. As an adult, he decided a sex change would solve his problems. Before the sex reassignment surgery could occur, Sy needed to live as a woman for two years. At the eighteen-month mark, the Lord got a hold of him, and he was reborn as a child of God. Sy stopped the procedure, embraced his masculinity, and pursued God.

The fanfare surrounding celebrity transgender individuals will fade away, but their pain will not. Whatever led them to decide upon reassignment has not been addressed. Surgery, implants, and hormones are all bandages to a complex physiological problem. Many seeking a new sexual identity have suffered severe emotional, physical, or sexual abuse.

Formerly, Johns Hopkins was the go-to place for sex reassignment surgeries. Many years of research have shown the surgery doesn't fix the struggler's core issues. The doctors at Johns Hopkins contend the issues are internal not external. Mental not physical. Johns Hopkins no longer participates in gender transitioning.

We are all born with or develop preferences and orientations. There are reasons for our struggles, but we all need to be reborn. Those of us who do not wrestle with the heartache of gender confusion have a choice. We can either help bring someone to God or push him further away from the Lord. Kindness and compassion are the answer. Prayer is the action.

Rather than condemning or celebrating those who have or are considering gender reassignment, let's pray for them. Pray for the healing only God can bring to such a devastating struggle. Pray the Lord draws each one to himself. And while you are on your knees, pray for my daughter, too.[5]

THE SWEET COMMUNION: HOW TO PRAY

All is not lost. The most powerful tool in the universe is still at our disposal—prayer. God is not surprised by our children's choice to identify as homosexuals. He expects us to bring this issue, as we should be bringing all the issues of our lives, before him. Here are some prayer starters based upon God's own words on the subject.

Based upon Leviticus 18:22

- *Lord God, I am bringing_____ to you today. Please deliver my child from the practice of homosexuality. Your Word says "having sex with another man as with a woman ... is a detestable sin." Make your desire for the heterosexual expression of sexuality clear to my child. In Jesus's strong name, Amen.*

Based upon Romans 1:21–32

Dear Lord God,

I'm here to talk to you about _____. Please do not abandon her to her homosexual desires. Cause my daughter to stay true to the natural desire you created in her as a girl instead of indulging in sex with another woman. Please free her from burning with lust for another woman. Keep her from shameful things with other women. Save her from suffering within herself the penalty such sin brings. Show her how to acknowledge you with her sexuality. Please do not abandon her to foolish thinking. Protect her from doing sexual acts with other women which should never be a part of her memory.

And as for my son, ignite the desire in him to have sexual relations with a woman (his wife). Please free him from burning with lust for another man. Keep him from shameful things with other men. Save him from suffering within himself the penalty such sin brings. Show him how to acknowledge you with his sexuality. Please do not abandon him to foolish thinking. Protect him from doing sexual acts with other men that should never a part of his memory.

In Jesus's strong name, Amen.

Based upon 1 Corinthians 6:9–10

Dear Lord God, please open _____'s eyes to the fact "those who do wrong will not inherit the kingdom of God." Do not let_____ be fooled. Make _____'s heart to understand "those who indulge in sexual sin, or who worship idols, or commit adultery, or are male prostitutes, or practice homosexuality, or are thieves, or greedy people, or drunkards, or are abusive, or cheat people—none of these will inherit the kingdom of God."

In Jesus's strong name, Amen.

Based upon Mark 9:14–29

Dear Lord God, _____ has a deceiving spirit causing an inability to hear your truth and speak the true nature of the need. In a real sense, _____ is deaf and mute, unable to hear from your word. _____ cannot say in agreement with your Word what you say about homosexuality. This spirit has seized my child and has thrown _____ into the gay life. _____ becomes rigid when we talk. I am bringing _____ to you to break the yoke which has prevailed since childhood. You can do anything. Please have compassion on us and help us.

Dear God, I am crying out! I believe; help my unbelief! Please God, in the name of Jesus, call out the deaf and mute spirit. Please do not let it enter _____ ever again. Cause _____ to be dead to homosexuality and ever more and more alive to you. Take my child's hand and raise _____ up to new life in you.

In Jesus's strong name, Amen.

In the first chapter of this book, I presented three scenes from the Bible of parents taking their young children to Jesus for his help. In the third scene, a young man couldn't extract himself from a problem that had taken over his body. After Jesus healed the young man, he told the father this kind of problem can only be rectified "by prayer and fasting" (Mark 9:29). In light of Jesus's instruction to the father, consider fasting periodically about this issue.

THE SUPPORTIVE CONNECTIONS:
WHERE TO TURN FOR ADDITIONAL HELP

Websites

Exchange Ministries–https://exchangeministries.org/. The stated mission of this organization is "to provide inspiration, hope, and refuge to those seeking to re-align their sexual identity with their identity in Christ through equipping and supporting the church, individuals, and families of LGBTQ+ identified loved ones."

Sex Change Regret—https://sexchangeregret.com/.

Stained Glass Rainbows—http://stainedglassrainbows.com/.

Books

For Men:

Growth into Manhood by Alan Medinger

You Don't Have to Be Gay: Hope and Freedom for Males Struggling with Homosexuality, or for Those Who Know of Someone Who Is by Jeff Konrad

Pursuing Sexual Wholeness: How Jesus Heals the Homosexual by Andrew Comiskey

For Women:

Restoring Sexual Identity: Hope for Women Who Struggles with Same-Sex Attraction by Anne Paulk

Out of Egypt: Leaving Lesbianism Behind by Jeannette Howard

Emotional Dependency by Lori Rentzel

Homosexuality: A New Christian Ethic by Elizabeth Moberly

The Heart of Female Same-Sex Attraction: A Comprehensive Counseling Resource by Janelle Hallman

For Parents, Loved Ones, Friends:

When Homosexuality Hits Home: What to Do When a Loved One Says, "I'm Gay" by Joe Dallas

Someone I Love is Gay: How Family and Friends Can Respond by Anita Worthen and Bob Davies

A Parent's Guide to Preventing Homosexuality by Joseph Nicolosi and Linda Ames Nicolosi

For Church Leaders:

Turning Controversy into Church Ministry by W. P. Campbell

For All:

Compassion Without Compromise: How the Gospel Frees Us to Love Our Gay Friends Without Losing the Truth By Adam T. Barr, Ron Citlau.

Gay Girl, Good God: The Story of Who I Was and Who God Has Always Been by Jackie Hill Perry.

Articles and Films

"Leaving the Gay Life Behind Worship." Artist B. David had an abusive childhood and ended up in a gay lifestyle. But an encounter with God changed him forever. *Christianity Today,* Andrew Greer/September 15, 2009, http://www.christianitytoday.com/ct/2009/septemberweb-only/bdavid-sep09.html.

"New Film Shows How to Leave the Gay Life Behind," Austin Ruse http://www.crisismagazine.com/2014/bounty-everlasting-hills-leaving-gay-life-behind.

"Ex-gay man: 'Homosexuality is just another human brokenness'" https://www.lifesitenews.com/news/ex-gay-homosexuality-is-just-another-human-brokenness.

Lori Wildenberg website and blog. Helping families build connections that last a lifetime.

https://loriwildenberg.com/2015/06/15/bruce-jenner-chaz-bono-and-my-oldest-daughter/

—CHAPTER 4—
I NO LONGER WANT TO LIVE

THE SIMILAR CHRONICLES: YOU ARE NOT ALONE

LENA'S STORY

Everything was going just fine in my life. I was a wife and mother of eight—three boys and two girls I birthed, and three stepdaughters. Darren was my youngest son. My husband, his stepdad, was a military man and ran a tight ship with lots of rules, most of which Darren didn't like, so the two of them seldom saw eye-to-eye. Still, Darren was never disrespectful and always did what he was told to do. He knew the Lord and attended church and Sunday school without any fuss. I loved him, would listen to him, and as with all my children, I thought I could always tell when something was bothering him.

When Darren was twenty, I noticed he was very anxious to be out on his own. He took advantage of an opportunity to leave home when he visited my mom in Bogalusa, Louisiana. He met a young lady who had her own place, so Darren called me, told me he was in love, and moved in with her. I tried to talk him out of the move, especially since the young lady was carrying their baby, but he insisted everything was fine. He got a job, and after the baby was born, he even asked me to name his daughter. He and I talked on the phone every week, and although this wasn't the best situation, he was an adult, so what could I do? He seemed happy so I decided to be happy for him.

Then came June 25, 1983, and life as I knew it changed. I arrived home from work to a house surrounded by cars. *What did my husband have going on? Must be another evening of the kids over for him to cook dinner for them the way he liked to do.* But when I walked in the house, everyone sitting around was looking sad. Then I started scanning to room to see if anyone was missing. *Were the grandkids okay? What was going on?*

As I sat on the sofa, my husband yelled to my oldest son, "Tell her! Please tell her!"

"Tell me what? You tell me. Somebody tell me something!"

My son wrapped me in his arms as he cried, "Darren is dead. He committed suicide."

I just remember screaming and falling to the floor. *How did I not know my child was in this much pain? I talked to him two days ago and he sounded fine. God, how could you let this happen to my sweet, twenty-one-year-old son? What was going to happen to Darren's soul? Will he go to hell because he killed himself?*

A myriad of questions flooded my mind. Then came the whys and the need to know exactly what happened. I learned Darren and the young lady had broken up, and she had started seeing someone else. Evidently, it was too much for him. He must have really wanted to die because he not only hung himself with his belt, but he had also turned on the gas, so if one method failed, the other would finish the job.

My next reaction was to place blame. I blamed the young lady and refused to talk to her. He'd still be alive if she had loved my son like my son loved her. I blamed my husband. Maybe if he hadn't been so hard on Darren, he would have come home when things went bad instead of ending his life.

I blamed myself. How could I have not known my own flesh and blood needed me? Why wasn't I there for him?

My blame game led to anger and self-imposed isolation. For six months, I went to work, went home, cooked dinner, and went to bed. I hardly talked to anyone. I hated myself. I hated I hadn't had a chance to hold Darren and tell him how much I loved him and how important he was to me. My mind was stuck on the fact no mother should ever have to bury her child. I was a mess. Later, my other children told me how abandoned they felt. They had lost both their brother and their mother. Now on top of being sad, I was failing them too.

Two years after Darren's death, a couple of ladies from my church began to minister to me and put me back on the right path. I received the counsel I needed and found the ability to forgive everyone—the young lady, my husband, Darren, and even myself. I begged God to heal my broken heart and trusted him to wipe away all my tears. I don't know what my son's last words were to God, but I do know our salvation, even Darren's, is God's business and is based upon grace by faith alone, not works (See Ephesians 2:8–9).

THE STRESSFUL COMPLICATION: THE ISSUE

As we read Lena's account of her son Darren's suicide, our hearts go out to her. We can also learn from her story.

THE SIGNS

We may not always notice or be aware of the warning signals someone is contemplating suicide. When we're separated by many miles, as Lena was, we may not be able to recognize nonverbal clues, and emotions may be masked over the phone lines. Do not take on the guilt of not seeing or responding to signs you were not close enough to see.

According to the American Foundation for Suicide Prevention (AFSP), the most common warning signs given by a suicidal individual fall into three categories—talk, behavior, and mood. If you are in the presence of your son or daughter regularly, pay close attention and get help for your children if they talk about:

- Killing themselves
- Feeling hopeless
- Having no reason to live
- Being a burden to others
- Feeling trapped
- Unbearable pain[1]

The AFSP website also lists "behaviors that may signal risk, especially if related to a painful event, loss, or change."

- Increased use of alcohol or drugs
- Looking for a way to end their lives, such as searching online for methods
- Withdrawing from activities
- Isolating from family and friends
- Sleeping too much or too little
- Visiting or calling people to say goodbye
- Giving away prized possessions
- Aggression
- Fatigue[2]

Finally, "people who are considering suicide often display one or more of the following moods:"

- Depression
- Anxiety
- Loss of interest
- Irritability
- Humiliation/Shame
- Agitation/Anger
- Relief/Sudden Improvement[3]

Family is important, and relationships are worth nurturing. Isolation allows room for errant thoughts, and those wandering, lonely thoughts could turn to suicidal ones. There is merit in working hard at keeping the lines of communication open when our young adults leave home. They still need us, just in different ways than they did when they were younger. We won't know what they are thinking unless we are talking regularly about what's on their minds. They need to continue to feel secure enough in their relationship with us to know they can come to us with anything and everything.

The young adult years are confusing. The popularity of the relatively new phenomenon of "adulting courses" online and as podcasts, proves our adult children want to be successful grown-ups. They are realizing there is much they don't know and possibly can't handle. Our kids who find coping difficult may turn to unhealthy solutions if they feel disclosure of their real thoughts will be met with anger, disapproval, ridicule, or dismissal. Remember, as with us, our young adults' feelings are real, and even if we disagree, those feelings must be approached with respect and honesty.

Regardless, we must remain real and honest. It's important to be careful not to become people we are not. Practice mutual respect. Our children want the freedom to express themselves freely—we deserve the same freedom. Agree we can both communicate everything, including disapproval or disagreement, calmly and without disdain in our voice or manner. They can say exactly what they want us to hear, and we can say exactly what we want them to hear. The foundation for open communication is the fact family is important, and you care deeply about each other.

LOVE HURTS

Love can hurt. Thanks to the freedom and availability of an incredible number of social media sites, young adults nowadays are privy to many types of love relationships, but at the core of them all is the idea of commitment. Teddy Pendergrass sang on his R & B album in 1978 asserting the best feeling ever is to love someone and receive love from them. When Darren and his lady-friend broke up, his heart broke, and the pain was something he'd never felt before. He couldn't see one day past it. Unfortunately, Darren didn't afford anyone a chance to show him tomorrows do come on the other side of lost loves.

If given the opportunity, we ought to take the time to legitimize our children's sorrow when a relationship goes awry, but also offer hope for tomorrow. Don't allow depressing thoughts to linger. Visit, call, email, text, send Facebook messages. We should do whatever we have to do to keep tabs on our young adults' state of mind. It's also a great idea to talk through how break-ups can be devastating when they enter their first serious relationship.

I remember being devastated when my break-ups occurred. I may not have felt like dying, but I sure cried a lot because of the pain. Have you ever shared one of your break-up stories with your kids? There's entertainment for sure, but sharing your vulnerable, human side will open deeper vistas of understanding between you and your child.

SUICIDE IS SEPARATION, NOT A SOLUTION

We've probably all heard the phrase—suicide is a permanent solution to a temporary problem. This may sound trite, but it's true. Suicide separates more than the person from all other family members. A child's death by suicide can cause parents to withdraw from each other and their other children, and siblings can find their grief isolates them from each other as well. The immediate family may be estranged from extended family members and friends because no one knows what to say or how to act in the aftermath of the loss. Whatever problems existed prior to the death are not solved—they are merely transferred and amplified to all those left behind.

Although all the above is true, your suicidal child does not understand any of it. The focus is on separation from the pain. All they know is something must be done to relieve the pain, and they believe doing something is better than doing nothing. The thinking is doing something which cannot be reversed must be better than the pain. Anything to make the pain stop. It's imperative for your child to come to see—first, they're not the only one who has ever felt this way; and second, the hurt will diminish. There will be a little less pain every day, and there will most likely be new love along the way.

SUICIDE IS THE RESULT OF A PERSON'S PAIN ONLY

Suicide is about the person who commits the act. No one else. We should neither blame someone else nor carry the fault on our own shoulders. A suicidal person's pain is their own. They hurt. They are in a depressed state and experiencing anxiety. They are drowning—feeling lost, isolated, and hopeless. We are on the outside, many times not even able to empathize because our own experiences, although similar, can never be someone else's. Breakthrough is possible, but realize the suicidal person must be the one who allows the door to open, even if only a tiny crack. Our young adult children are responsible for their decisions, including the decision to end their lives.

GRIEF IS ENHANCED BY BLAME AND GUILT

The crushing grief of losing a child to suicide is magnified when we insist upon piling blame and guilt on top of our grieving. Placing blame seems only natural, but it is not necessary. We must be watchful and avoid transferring our grief. As much as we would like the grief to go away, it will not. We must travel through it. God will hold our hand and when necessary, he will carry us. Use Jesus instead of blame and guilt as a buffer against the grief. Accept grief as the natural response to the sudden death of a beloved child. God, in his mercy, will carry us to deeper depths in him, depths only available to those deeply suffering. As Corrie ten Boom, celebrated author of *The Hiding Place*, learned in the Nazi prison camp, "There is no pit so deep that my God is not deeper still."[4]

THE SAVIOR'S COMMUNICATION:
THE BIBLE'S MESSAGE

The most gripping point for Christian parents is the question of whether our children go to heaven or hell if they perform this as their last act on earth. This question has been debated by qualified theologians over the years. The answer depends solely upon the truth about how we obtain salvation in the first place. Ephesians 2:8–9 states, "For by grace you have been saved through faith, and that not of yourselves; it is the gift of God, not of works, lest anyone should boast". And Romans 10:9–10 adds "if you confess with your mouth the Lord Jesus and believe in your heart that God has raised Him from the dead, you will be saved. For with the heart one believes unto righteousness, and with the mouth confession is made unto salvation". First John 5:11–12 makes the point even more clear, "And this is what God has testified: He has given us eternal life, and this life is in his Son. Whoever has the Son has life; whoever does not have God's Son does not have life" (NLT).

Our salvation comes to us by Christ alone. We don't deserve it and can't earn it. We don't work to get it, and we don't work to keep it. No act or work on our part produces the salvation God offers. The cake has already been made, and it's free. But we must eat. Once we eat—once we open the door of our hearts—Jesus floods in. Through Jesus, God loves us, and we can't make him stop. So, just as no act or work on our part produces salvation, no act or work on our part can erase salvation.

Do we become sinless once we have Christ in our hearts? No, but we ought to sin less. The forgiveness of our sins is once for all—past, present, and future. There is no need to run to the altar every church service to get saved again because we sinned during the week. We would never leave the sanctuary if that were the case. We should ask God to forgive us for known sins as we continue living, but our sin—the nature born in us, which originally separated us from God—was taken care of at the cross.

None of us know whether the last thought, word, or deed of our earthly existence will be a holy one. Thank God our passage into heaven is not predicated upon what we think, say, or do, but upon what Jesus has already done. For believers, if our last thought is ungodly, and then we die, the thought is covered by the blood of the Lamb. If our last word is one which would have gotten our mouths washed out with soap, the word is covered by the blood. If our last act results in our death, the act is covered by the blood. Is it right to think wrong thoughts, say bad words, or end one's own life? No. Do these acts, committed by a believer cancel salvation? Listen to Jesus's own explanation: "Every sin and blasphemy can be forgiven—except blasphemy against the Holy Spirit, which will never be forgiven. Anyone who speaks against the Son of Man can be forgiven, but anyone who speaks against the Holy Spirit will never be forgiven, either in this world or in the world to come" (Matthew 12:31–32 NLT). In short, blasphemy against the Holy Spirit is the refusal to yield to God through Jesus Christ. Therefore, the only thing keeping us from salvation is our death with a heart yet separated from God. And our loving God knows, cares for, and fully understands hearts desperate for relief from unbearable pain.

Rarely is anyone else present when people die by their own hand. We are completely unable to know whether the act was accompanied by a fist-to-the-clouds declaration against God. I remember hearing the black box recording of the cockpit conversation as a doomed aircraft plummeted from the sky. A string of venomous curse words against the Father God streamed from the pilot's mouth. Perhaps in this case, the state of the pilot's afterlife seems pretty sure and dismal. According to Jesus's words in Matthew 12:31–32 quoted above, blasphemy against the Holy Spirit—the out-and-out rejection and repudiation of God's work in Christ—is the only thing, according to Jesus, which will keep us out of heaven, and I think Jesus would know.

Let's not, however, be unbalanced and take suicide lightly. Suicide is complicated. As much as we would like to understand the inner thoughts of a person considering suicide, we must remember the mental, emotional, physical, psychological, and even economic state of the person combine to move them to make such a drastic decision. In many cases, a perfect storm evolves when several or all these factors are negative at the same time, thus producing suicidal thoughts and plans.

So, what's the answer to the question, "Did my child's suicide nullify salvation?" Some denominations hold salvation can be lost by a final act like suicide. Others seriously doubt the commitment of people who lose all hope and decide to end their lives. Nevertheless, the Bible supports the fact if the person was indeed saved, no devil in hell, nor any personal act brought about even in the depths of depression, can rip their soul from the hands of God. "For I am persuaded," says the apostle Paul, "that neither death nor life, nor angels nor principalities nor powers, nor things present nor things to come, nor height nor depth, nor any other created thing, shall be able to separate us from the love of God which is in Christ Jesus our Lord" (Romans 8:38–39).

THE SINCERE CARE-FRONTATION

Sadly, there is nothing we can do to reverse reality after a suicide attempt is successful. Traveling through the stages of grief is difficult but is necessary and healthy. God will prove to be strength in your weakness and light in your utter darkness. You are not at fault. God loved your child, and he loves you.

If, however, your child is still living, how do you care for and confront your young adult daughter or son who considers suicide? Everything I found in my research instructs us to move into action when we suspect a child is seriously thinking about suicide. Doing nothing is not an option. Throw finesse out the window. There is no need to be harsh, but we must be direct. Asking, "Are you thinking about killing yourself?" does not increase the chances your child will follow through. You are not placing the idea in their head. You are calling attention to the peril just like you would do with any other imminent danger. You are also letting them know they're not on an island alone with the pain.

Do all you can to keep your child safe if you sense the threat of carrying out the suicide attempt is indeed imminent. Do not leave them alone. Disable to access to lethal items. If they get mad at you, so be it. Mad is breathing. As soon as possible, get help from a trained professional. Your child may even need to be hospitalized until the crisis has passed. This is no time to be embarrassed or to hesitate because you are worrying about what people might say or think. Let them talk. You need for your child to be alive.

Be available to listen, really listen. Struggle to find the fine line between being too pushy and too standoffish. To help the conversation along, an article by the Mayo Clinic staff suggests asking questions like:

- How are you coping with what's been happening in your life?
- Do you ever feel like giving up?
- Have you ever thought about suicide before, or tried to harm yourself before?

The Mayo Clinic article goes on to suggest you "ask the person directly about his or her feelings, even though it may be awkward. Listen to what the person has to say and take it seriously. Just talking to someone who really cares can make a big difference."[6]

As you listen to your child, acknowledge and respect the words you hear. Do not get sucked into lies but listen openly to what your child believes to be true. Now is not the time to be argumentative, to split hairs, or try to "win" a war of words. Your "win" is one more day and a step back from the suicidal edge. Your child is a grown-up with grown-up problems. You may have handled the same problem differently, but you are not your child.

So again, listen. Care-frontation requires a humble stance and admitting you don't understand but you sincerely want to. This is not about you. This is about your child who is in such distress, believing the only way to stop the pain is to die has been internalized. Your precious offspring sees no alternative. Silently and respectfully allow your child to express feelings without judgment—if not to you to someone else who cares and who will give your child the opportunity to hear the feelings said aloud. Actively listen by adding none of your own ideas. If you say anything, simply reflect back what has been said so your child will know for sure you are listening.

In the event your child refuses to talk to you, enlist others to be listening ears needed. Don't get your feelings hurt—just remember the bottom line is to get your child to express feelings so, eventually, they will see tomorrow is worth living for. You'll then have the hope of the all-important next day to build, develop, and strengthen your relationship.

THE SWEET COMMUNION: HOW TO PRAY

As always, God hears the prayers of an honest heart. His shoulders are big enough and strong enough to handle whatever you have to say. So, go ahead, get it all out. Journal, cry, scream, point your finger—tell God everything inside you. He loves you, and he wants this interaction. Remember, just like you want him to listen to you, he wants you to listen to him in return. Once you've finished with your own words, use his to pray about your suicidal young adult. Prayers based on Scripture focus your thoughts away from the problem and onto the solution found in Christ alone. Fill your son's or daughter's name in below. Here are two samples to get you started:

PRAYER #1

Dear God,

Psalm 36:7 says, "How precious is your lovingkindness, O God! Therefore, the children of men put their trust under the shadow of your wings." I know your lovingkindness extends to _____. You think precious thoughts about _____. Help _____ to put complete trust in you. Help _____ hide under the shadow of your wings—in a protected space shutting out all thoughts of suicide. Thank you, God.

In Jesus's majestic and powerful name, Amen.

PRAYER #2

Dear God,

Psalm 78:5–7 declares you "appointed a law— your word—in Israel, which [you] commanded our fathers, that they should make them known to their children." The law was "that the generation to come might know [your word], the children who would be born, that they may arise and declare [your word] to their children, that they may set their hope in God, and not forget the works of God, but keep His commandments." I ask, God, you bring to _____'s remembrance the words poured in during childhood pertaining to knowledge and belief about you and your word. Flood _____'s aching soul with the truth of your word which says, "For God so loved the world that He gave His only begotten son" for everyone. Eradicate thoughts of suicide so _____ will stand on your word in order to arise and declare your word to the generations to come. Give _____ a future beyond today's pain. Day by day, encourage and comfort _____ with your word allowing _____ to put hope in you. Remind _____ of all the blessings you supply each and every day—blessings to dwarf the current pain. And move _____ to keep your commandments.
In Jesus's precious and holy name, Amen.

Choose other Scripture passages to personalize and pray back to God. A great place to find Scriptures to mirror your concerns is in the book of Psalms, but don't hesitate to use Scriptures from any of the other sixty-five books. The prayers of the people in the Bible probably say a lot of what you want to say to God.

THE SUPPORTIVE CONNECTIONS:
WHERE TO TURN FOR ADDITIONAL HELP

LIVE HELP

National Suicide Prevention Lifeline

The website home page says: No matter what problems you are dealing with, we want to help you find a reason to keep living. By calling 1-800-273-TALK (8255) you'll be connected to a skilled, trained counselor at a crisis center in your area, anytime 24/7. https://nicic.gov/national-suicide-prevention-lifeline

WEBSITES

American Foundation for Suicide Prevention (AFSP), https://afsp.org/

Suicide Prevention Resource Center https://www.sprc.org/

Suicide Awareness Voice of Education (SAVE) heeps://save.org/ (SAVE has resources for attempt survivors)

BOOKS

Too Soon to Say Goodbye. Susan Titus Osborn, Karen L. Kosman, and Jeenie Gordon.

Preventing Suicide: A Handbook for Pastors, Chaplains and Pastoral Counselors. Karen Mason.

Hello, I Want to Die Please Fix Me: Depression in the First Person. Anna Mehler Paperny.

—CHAPTER 5—
I'M MOVING IN WITH MY BOYFRIEND/ GIRLFRIEND

THE SIMILAR CHRONICLES: YOU'RE NOT ALONE

REVA'S STORY

I stepped off the curb and opened the car door. Valerie, my oldest daughter, followed me. She stopped me before I could get into the driver's seat. "Mom, I just want you to know, Jake and I are moving in together."

I gasped for air and grabbed the door frame to steady myself. It may have been easier to breathe if a professional linebacker had targeted me in the gut. This kind of thing happens in other people's families, not in ours. My husband and I had always made sure our children knew the right thing to do and loved God in the process.

Finally regaining enough air to talk, I stammered, "But … but … Val, you know that's not what we have taught you. You know that is wrong, so wrong." A tear escaped and people coming out of the drugstore we had just exited became a blur.

"Mom, I know what I am doing. It's okay. Jake and I love each other."

"Love? You can't possibly know what real love is. And you know it is wrong to live with anyone before marriage."

"Mom, you can't change my mind. Jake and I have decided to start our lives together."

My daughter was twenty years old and a good college student. You would think she could make better decisions. But she no longer wanted to follow the rules her father and I had established. There was nothing we could do.

As days and weeks went by, I fervently prayed for my daughter and Jake. All I kept hearing in my spirit was God's voice repeating over and over to me, "Just love her, just love her." *Really? Do you know how hard that is, God, when I want to show her the right way to live?* He wouldn't answer my longing cries—he would only repeat, "Just love her."

Valerie withdrew from the family and spent all her time in her apartment with Jake about fifty miles away. I called regularly but every time got her answering machine. With caller ID, she could choose whether to answer my calls. Although she rarely answered, each time I called, I left a simple message. "I love you." As I prayed for my daughter, I wanted to be close to her. Many times, I got into the car and drove to her apartment complex so I could sit in the parking lot and pray.

Weeks turned into months, then one day Valerie and Jake came to visit. Jake looked at Valerie's father and said, "I'd like to talk to you, Sir."

The two of them went outside while Val and I washed the supper dishes. When they came back in, my husband came over to the sink, and Valerie went into the den with Jake. "He wants to marry her," John whispered.

"There's no way I want him for a son-in-law. I have prayed for her mate since the day she was born. He's not the one."

"Well, she thinks he is. I agree with you, but this is our daughter's choice. We are going to have to support her and let God love them through us."

After that night, unanswered phone calls continued for a while, but as the wedding date drew closer, we began talking a bit more. Valerie bubbled with excitement, but I went to bed with a sore tongue for having bitten it so hard during our conversations.

They married and moved even farther away. I continued to pray and ask God to protect her and to one day bring her back to us. God continually reminded me he loved her even more than I did. I asked God to assure her of our love for her.

ANNETTE'S STORY

David, my middle son, moved thousands of miles away when he went to college. Although I trusted him, I knew his proclivity for having fun. I knew the college life could register in his mind as being "party central," and he could be drawn away from the need to buckle down to his studies. And then there were the beautiful young women he was bound to meet. Again, I had to trust his Christian upbringing would kick in and he'd be able to continue to distinguish right from wrong in the new relationships he would forge.

David made it through graduation, exiting in the funny hat and robe with a Bachelor of Science degree in business, despite all the fun he had. He'd kept his feet firmly on the ground, garnered several honor certificates, joined both a business and a service fraternity, served several successful internships, and was now headed into the rest of his adult life on an excellent note.

I cried like a baby the minute "Pomp and Circumstance" began to play at the ceremony.

He decided to take up residence in the state where he had gone to school, got a job, found an apartment, and joined a church. It was at church where he met the gorgeous Alexis. *Ah, graduation, a job, an apartment, a church home, and a Christian girl. What more could a mom dream for her son?* Alexis was sweet and beautiful inside and out. I fell in love with her immediately. She was the perfect choice, and she'd be the daughter I never had. My heart couldn't help but envision the proposal announcement, my day as mother of the groom, and stepping into my new role as mother-in-law. I planned to be the perfect one.

Imagine my dream bubble not just popping but exploding when instead of the expected announcement of upcoming wedding bells, David came by to tell me, "Mom, Alexis is pregnant." And then a month or so later, he informed me, "Mom, Alexis and I are moving in together. I need to be there for my child."

My thoughts swirled. *Yes, you do have to be there for your child, and I'm proud of you for that, but you also need to get married. You've complicated the issue, but that doesn't change God's position on shacking up.*

David's explanation wasn't working for me. He told me, "We need to get to know each other better before we get married and make that life commitment."

I couldn't hold my response. "David, you obviously *knew* each other (in the biblical sense) well enough to produce this baby. Part of stepping up to be a father includes stepping up to be the husband for your child's mother. Being a husband is supposed to precede being a father. You flipped the script—now it's not okay to ignore part one because you pressed on to part two."

David knew they had made a mistake in having sex and getting pregnant before they were married. He also insisted he and Alexis didn't want to make another mistake and get married if they weren't compatible. They needed time to work and pray through the entire situation. As much as I wanted to resist it, the issue didn't seem as black and white anymore. They were being responsible as far as the child was concerned. I had to let them be adults, parents, and Christians, working out their relationships with each other and with God. He and Alexis moved in together, and we all prepared ourselves to welcome the precious baby who would soon come into the world.

THE STRESSFUL COMPLICATION: THE ISSUE

The issue before us is whether it is right or wrong for a couple to live together before they get married. Let's be honest—our society just does not see anything wrong with this anymore. Ironically, David (from the story of David and Alexis above) had always vowed he would not "play house" with some girl before marriage, but the baby changed everything as babies are known to do.

Still, even without a baby in the picture, many young couples not only think it's okay to live together before marriage but believe it would be irresponsible *not* to do so. This practice is, in part, the reason for the decline in divorce rates over the past ten years.[1] What's happening? First, young people, many of whom grew up in single parent homes possibly due to the divorce of their parents, are opting out of marriage in the first place. Second, they reason that, if their "holy" parents couldn't make it by doing things "right," why should they think they can just jump the broom and live happily ever after without taking a test run at marriage by living together first. However, if they do decide to get married to the person with whom they are cohabiting, studies still show that premarital cohabitation is associated with greater odds of divorce.[2]

This argument seems to pose a problem for Christian parents whether the parents have been divorced or not. What is left to say when an argument sounds logical and plausible, is communicated by our thoughtful and intelligent young adults, and the societal statistics seem to agree with them?

THE SAVIOR'S COMMUNICATION:
THE BIBLE'S MESSAGE

There are no verses in the Bible that say, "Thou shalt not shack up." We need to understand, though, the Bible speaks to every human situation if not by precept, then by principle. Living together before marriage is such a case.

God's plan for us is that we would mirror his character to the world. To do that, we must reflect God's uniqueness. Many things make God unique, but one of his overarching characteristics is his holiness. His holiness influences the way he deals with us. Therefore, to look like a holy God, we must live as holy people.

This is not a new idea. As the Israelites traveled toward the promised land, God instructed them saying, "When you enter the land the LORD your God is giving you, be very careful not to imitate the detestable customs of the nations living there" (Deuteronomy 18:9 NLT). What the culture practiced was to have no bearing upon nor exert influence over what God's people did or how God's people acted.

Let's just be honest: A young couple in love will be sexually attracted to each other. Living together makes fornication too easy. Matthew 26:41 gives us practical, down-to-earth advice. "Keep watch and pray, so that you will not give in to temptation. For the spirit is willing, but the body is weak!" (NLT). And the Scriptures cannot get much clearer than the words found in 1 Corinthians 6:18 which tells us straight out to "run from sexual sin! No other sin so clearly affects the body as this one does. For sexual immorality is a sin against your own body" (NLT).

The issue here is the fact that living together outside of marriage puts our young adults into a situation of snubbing their noses at God's direct command to abstain from fornication—the Bible's term for the act of sexual intercourse between people who are not married to each other. Couples who want to honor God with their lives must abstain from sexual relations until they are legally married.

THE SINCERE CARE-FRONTATION

So, how do you care for and confront your young adult children who plan to cohabit with their girlfriend or boyfriend? As with every situation covered in this book, a parent's approach means everything. Outright condemnation never builds bridges. Our children will probably be more willing to receive our honesty if communicated with love.

Start out by listening. This is the best way to let your children know you genuinely care for and respect them. Young adults who respect their Christian parents already have a good idea of how you will feel about the announcement of their plans to move in with their boyfriend or girlfriend. What are their reasons for making this move? Listen. Really listen without building your comeback arguments in your mind as they talk.

When it's your turn to talk, repeat to your children what they have just said to you to be sure you understand their reasons. Allow them to explain anything they feel you do not understand. Not until they are comfortable that you fully understand their point of view can you begin to share your ideas.

Start by stating your desire for harmony. Communicate you sincerely long to maintain a vital relationship with them even through times of disagreement. Thank them for sharing their inner thoughts and plans with you and for trusting you to take them seriously. Now it is safe for you share your thoughts and concerns.

Begin with practical points. Discuss how much they've thought about everything involved in trying to blend two lives together without the safety net of a legal bond and total commitment. Some discussion starters could be questions and comments like the following:

- How does your boyfriend or girlfriend's family feel about the move you two are about to make?

- Financial issues can cause many problems when people live together.

- Who is paying the rent on your residence? In whose name is the rental agreement? What will happen to this agreement if one of you decides to leave the relationship? Are you furnishing the apartment together?

- How are the two of you handling the other financial issues about things you must share: food, utilities, trash collection, taxes, insurance, emergencies (an appliance breaks down, cars need repair, someone has a medical crisis, etc.)?

- Is the marriage conversation on the table?

- What are you doing to grow closer to the Lord together?

- Since I know you are believers who desire to honor God, how are you planning to abstain from sexual relations until you get married? If you are not planning to abstain, can you justify this decision with Scripture?

- What will you do if you become pregnant?

One couple I know visited with their daughter and her boyfriend when the youngsters announced they would move in together. Although I do not know if the above questions were part of the conversation, they had a respectful conversation. In addition, the parents had prayed about presenting an alternate possibility.

In this situation, the young couple had decided they were going to get married in the future, but they wanted a particular type of wedding and knew it would take months, maybe even a year or more, before they could amass the money it would take to have the blow-out wedding they wanted. The parents suggested they get married privately at the justice of the peace. Then they could live together without sinning sexually while they saved money and planned the ceremony and reception of their dreams. The wedding did not have to be a ceremony marking the beginning of their lives together. The ceremony and party would simply be a big, shared celebration of their love.

This approach demonstrated that honoring God must be more important than anything even as it applies to this very practical area of our lives. It is possible to get to know each other and save money without living in the same apartment or house. No, you may not know all your mate's intimate habits before you live together, but that's part of the fun of sharing a whole lifetime together as you learn and grow together as husband and wife. If you are patient and observant, you can get to know a person's character without marrying each other. God will honor obedience as he does whenever we choose to obey him.

THE SWEET COMMUNION: HOW TO PRAY

When God is honored, he has a way of turning our mess-ups into miracles. Place your son's or daughter's names and the names of the girlfriend or boyfriend in the following prayers.

Dear God,

We thank you for your wonderful idea of marriage and making it and the marriage bed honorable in your eyes. We are also grateful that you give your favor to a young man who finds a wife, his "good

*thing." We pray that _____(son/daughter)_____
and __(girlfriend/boyfriend)_____ will live in
your honor and favor and get married before they
begin to live together as husband and wife. God
will judge the sexually immoral and adulterous. We
pray that ___(male)_____ will live showing honor
to __(female)_____, since they are heirs with you of
the grace of life and their prayers would be effective.
(Hebrews 13:4, Proverbs 18:22, Genesis 2:24, I Peter
3:7)*

*We also pray, Lord, that _____and
_____ will be able to realize whether
or not they are right for each other as they date. Help
_____ and _____ base
their decisions about each other on what your word
says about how mates ought to treat each other. Let
___(male)_____ see and treat ___(female)_____
as one of your precious daughters. Let __
(female)_____ see and treat ___(male)_____ as
a man of God. If _____ and _____
are having premarital sex, forgive them and lead
them to confess their sin and turn from it until they
lawfully marry. (2 Corinthians 6:14, Isaiah 55:7)
We are grateful that you love _____
__ and _____. As they move
toward marriage, knit their hearts in forever love for
each other. Help _____ to consistently love
_____ and provide for his family, as you
also help _____ to support _____
and respect him always. (John 3:16, 1 Timothy 5:8,
Ephesians 5:33)*

In Jesus's strong name, Amen.

Chapter Postscript

As a footnote, I'm sure you're curious about how each
situation from the beginning of this chapter worked out.
Sadly, Valerie's marriage to Jake landed her in an extremely
unhealthy relationship. They divorced, but several years

later, Valerie met and married a young man who loved both her and God very much. They're doing well.

David went to his pastor and told him of Alexis's pregnancy. He submitted himself to his pastor's counseling, and an older man in the church who had been through the same situation mentored David. Soon after the baby was born, David and Alexis decided to get married, and their little family has now grown to five.

Things do work out.

THE SUPPORTIVE CONNECTIONS:
WHERE TO TURN FOR ADDITIONAL HELP

A cohabitation agreement is a legal document permitting people who live together without marriage can be legally bound. The agreement provides for "the status, ownership, and division of property between them, including future property owned or to be acquired by either or both of them."[3] The document covers topics like property, debts, household expenses, etc.

I am not suggesting our young people use this document to legitimize their living together. I am mentioning it here because of the topics it covers. Perhaps the practical reality of talking through these items will help your son or daughter reconsider cohabitation.

Finally, Christian young adults want to please the Lord. Enlist pastoral counseling to help your son or daughter think through the decision to cohabitate.

—CHAPTER 6—
I'M LEAVING THE CHURCH (THE FAITH)

THE SIMILAR CHRONICLES: YOU ARE NOT ALONE

AMANDA'S STORY

We have a blended family. My husband and I raised all the kids in our home, although my kids from my first marriage could visit with their father, and my husband's kids from his first marriage could visit with their mother. We taught all our children how to live a biblical life and we also modeled the behavior as best we could. We were very active in our church and so were the kids. Unfortunately, the mother of my two stepchildren lived a life that included drug abuse and alcohol use. She tried her best to influence the children in negative ways. Even her relatives tried dissuading them from following our lifestyle even though we had our kids' best interest at heart by teaching them to avoid abusing illegal substances, alcohol, drugs, and other untoward behavior, and to love, honor, and follow God.

As the years passed, the kids grew into young adults and moved out. We felt comfortable they had embraced our faith for themselves. My husband's children had also become adept at avoiding controversial conversations comparing the differences between their parents' households.

Naturally, they still loved both of their parents, so it was understandable when my husband's son called us very upset one day to inform us that his mom was very ill. What I didn't see coming is what he said next. He stated he didn't understand how God is supposed to be so loving but would take his mom from him. He told us it was God's fault and he refused to believe in a God who would make his mom suffer and possibly die.

We tried to explain God gives us free will to make decisions, every decision has consequences, and his mom's lifestyle of drug use had led to her illness. We told him even though he doesn't believe in God, God believes in him, and loves him. We would continue to pray for him, but he didn't accept our words and the call ended.

Knowing our son has walked away from the faith is hurtful, but we also know we instilled the Word of God in him. He must have his own personal encounter with Jesus. We will just continue to love him and pray for him.

THE STRESSFUL COMPLICATION:
THE ISSUE/THE PROBLEM

Denouncing the faith is possibly the most serious problem this book will face because we're dealing here with the only eternal issue this book discusses. Refusing to trust in Jesus has grave consequences. We know that Acts 4:12 says, "Nor is there salvation in any other, for there is no other name under heaven given among men by which we must be saved."

Here's the dilemma. The pressure is on from our post-Christian society to allow children more and more autonomy to make their own choices in every area of life. It is a foregone conclusion that young children can be easily influenced. The world of marketing knows that. For example, walk down the cereal aisle the next time you're in a grocery store. Notice how all the sugary, "fun" cereals are at the eye level of a child who is riding in the basket seat. Those clever TV commercial jingles played repeatedly during Saturday morning cartoons trigger the nagging in the cereal aisle gets those boxes of cereal thrown into the cart despite their low nutritional value.

So, it is educational institutions, video games, TV shows, music, movies, social media messages, and even government agencies are feeding our kids messages about their right to make their own choices despite their parents' guidance and wishes.

For example, one of my friends took Lizzy, her twelve-year-old daughter, to her annual doctor's appointment. The doctor shut my friend, Lizzy's mother, out of the exam room stating Lizzy had the right to her medical privacy and the mother would have to get the daughter's approval to be present in the room while the doctor performed his examination and consultation. The doctor said he was mandated to protect Lizzy's privacy, especially as he would be having a conversation with her about having sex, sexually transmitted diseases, and birth control options.

The same type of thing happened with me and my son Matthew when he was a freshman in college. Matthew was rushed to the hospital and would have stayed there alone had he not been able to cry out for his mother. Neither the university nor the hospital could contact me without Matthew's permission since he was no longer a minor. The school could have been sued if they had divulged Matthew's medical condition.

Both Lizzy and Matthew needed their parents' wisdom regarding their health issues. They were not equipped to handle those situations on their own, and Lizzy and Matthew requested their parents' involvement. By the time our children are in their teens, and certainly by the time they are young adults, many have been swayed to believe there is no practical reason to adhere to their parents' advice, let alone the strict guidelines of organized religion or any one particular faith. Are children and kids in their early young adulthood in a position to discern between wise and foolish choices, especially regarding weighty matters such as dropping one's faith identification?

Paradigm Treatment, an organization whose medical and clinical teams address the root causes of the struggles young people face in today's stress-filled world, offers some insight into why teens make some of the choices they make. In explaining brain development, Paradigm Treatment says:

> One of the biggest differences researchers have found between adults and adolescents is the pre-frontal cortex. This part of the brain is still developing in teens and doesn't complete its growth until approximately early to midtwenties. The prefrontal cortex performs reasoning, planning, judgment, and impulse control, necessities for being an adult. Without the fully developed prefrontal cortex, a teen might make poor decisions and lack the inability to discern whether a situation is safe. Teens tend to experiment with risky behavior and don't fully recognize the consequences of their choices.
>
> On the other hand, in adults, the frontal cortex is completely developed. They are able to process and organize information. Adults, who are emotionally and psychologically healthy, can judge risky behavior and factor into decision-making the consequences of their choices. Teens might rely more on their amygdala, the part of the brain dealing with emotions, whereas adults rely more on their frontal cortex, leading to balanced thinking and behavior.[1]

The choice to identify with and follow the Christian faith comes along with indescribable benefits, some of which are not immediately discernable, and can be experienced at first only by faith. The choice to disassociate with the Christianity, however, comes along with invisible yet very real consequences that unfortunately can sneak up and catch one by surprise, and then it is everlastingly too late. Divorcing oneself from following God is not a decision the underdeveloped brain of a young adult is qualified to make.

Christian parents must come to terms with the reality of our belief system, realizing it will never be the popular choice, but is the eternally blessed one. We do not need to be aggressive or authoritarian to pass our faith on to our children. God is love and communicates his ways to us by love. We can do the same for our children, and we can trust that God loves them even more than we do. He is capable of keeping them even when they think they don't want to be kept.

THE SAVIOR'S COMMUNICATION: THE BIBLE'S MESSAGE

"For God so loved the world that He gave His only begotten Son, that whoever believes in Him should not perish but have everlasting life." John 3:16 could be the best-known Scripture. This verse is the super-condensed version of the Bible's whole theme and the reflection of the Father's heart. Further insight into just how God feels about all of us, including our children who turn from either the church or the faith, is found in the New Living Translation's rendering of 2 Peter 3:9. "The Lord isn't really being slow about his promise, as some people think. No, he is being patient for your sake. He does not want anyone to be destroyed but wants everyone to repent."

Despite what society says, it is the responsibility of all Christian parents to teach their children how to trust in God through Jesus Christ. A faith that does not wholeheartedly believe its own tenets is not much of a faith.

Since Old Testament times, parents have been directed to instruct their children about the faith. Deuteronomy 6:1 and 7 say, "Now this is the commandment, and these are the statutes and judgments which the LORD your God has commanded to teach you ... You shall teach them diligently to your children and shall talk of them when you sit in your house, when you walk by the way, when you lie down, and when you rise up." And Psalm 78:5 says, "For He established a testimony in Jacob, and appointed a law in Israel, which He commanded our fathers, that they should make them known to their children."

We're convinced we ought to teach our children God's statutes and judgments, but some may ask, "Well, there are so many. Which statutes and judgments am I required to teach?" All of them! However, the most important takeaway from God's Word is one I heard Dr. James Dobson say on his popular *Focus on the Family* radio show a few years ago. Just before his life-threatening surgery, he called his children to him and implored them, "Be sure to be there; just be there." God has made it abundantly clear about how to get to him. The Bible says:

> "There is no other name under heaven given among men by which we must be saved" (Acts 4:12).

> "Jesus said to him, "I am the way, and the truth, and the life. No one comes to the Father except through me" (John 14:6).

> "And this is the testimony, that God gave us eternal life, and this life is in his Son. Whoever has the Son has life; whoever does not have the Son of God does not have life" (1 John 5:11–12 ESV).

"If you confess with your mouth the Lord Jesus and believe in your heart that God has raised Him from the dead, you will be saved. For with the heart one believes unto righteousness, and with the mouth confession is made unto salvation" (Romans 10:9–10).

You probably have been teaching your child the right things about God. Your current dilemma is hearing their declaration they no longer believe in the church or have turned completely away from the faith. God is not surprised by your adult child's actions. He even has this under control and offers forgiveness and an escape for those who have turned their back on him. Colossians 1:21–23 states, "And you, who once were alienated and enemies in your mind by wicked works, yet now He has reconciled in the body of His flesh through death, to present you holy, and blameless, and above reproach in His sight—if indeed you continue in the faith, grounded and steadfast, and are not moved away from the hope of the gospel which you heard, which was preached to every creature under heaven, of which I, Paul, became a minister.

"As with the prodigal son's father in Luke chapter 15, God the Father is watching and waiting for your child to come home.

THE SINCERE CARE-FRONTATION

So how do you care for and confront your young adult son or daughter who has left or who plans to leave the faith?

Start by undergirding all your interactions with prayer. Never forget you are not in a physical struggle. Winning a person to the Lord involves spiritual warfare. I'm reminded of my friend's strong-willed three-year-old granddaughter who was being punished for some disobedience by being told to sit in the corner. She reluctantly stomped over to the time-out stool and plopped herself onto the seat as she announced, "But I'm standing up in my mind!" We cannot strong-arm another human being into the kingdom of God.

Maintain your familial love relationship with your child by doing all the regular, fun things families do together. It really is not necessary to drive home the message of salvation at a birthday party, a Fourth of July summer barbeque, a wedding reception, or a graduation party. Your desire is for harmony—for your son or daughter to be attracted to the image of Christ in you, not to be repelled by a false representation of the Lord's character they see in you.

Listen when you have the opportunity to talk with each other about faith. Ask with honest curiosity, "Why did you decide to leave the faith?" Resist thinking about all the ways you can negate every argument. Really listen to what's being said. Acknowledge your child's complaints as valid because how a person feels is how that person feels. We cannot tell our children they shouldn't feel their emotions, so listen to empathize. How would you react if you felt the same way your child feels?

Once you have listened, echo back what your young person just said to be sure you understand. Then ask for permission to respond. Adult conversations work by both people contributing, even if their ideas clash. If your child wants you to listen to and understand, you must be allowed to speak and be understood as well.

Of course, there is no way this book can chronicle all the possible reasons people turn their backs on Christianity, but several general themes seem to rise to the surface regularly.

PROBLEMS WITH PEOPLE

1. Young people are especially adept at seeing through folks who are disingenuous or inauthentic. The most important characteristic Christians should exhibit is

honesty. We must deal only with the truth when we try to represent to people the reality of our invisible God. Insincerity turns our kids off. They want no part of the faith if they have been hurt by insincere people who claim the name of Christ, because they associate him with such people.

2. A closely related complaint is the people-in-the-church-are-hypocrites reason. This reason varies slightly from the first. Hypocrites are church people who represent themselves as paragons of virtue but behind closed doors say or do things that reveal their sinful humanity.

3. Carmen recalls her first glimpse of hypocritical reality. At eighteen, she had been voted president of her national denomination's youth group. The new youth leadership team was taken to the hotel suite the conference was using for leadership meetings. When the door to the suite opened, she witnessed a scene she did not expect. The leading pastors, head deacons, and church board leaders were holding glasses of alcohol from the bar cart and filling the room with their cigarette and cigar smoke, all activities frowned upon by that particular denomination. This image did not square with her former picture of them wearing robes, sitting in the pulpit, preaching, and smiling to shake hands with parishioners at the door when the service was over.

Thankfully, this skewed peek into the real lives of those church leaders didn't turn Carmen away from the faith, but this kind of thing can send the message that church folks do not practice what they preach. If they aren't for real when they tell young people not to drink and smoke, how can their word be trusted on any matters they tell young people? By extension, why should the youth honor and obey God if their leaders don't?

A proper response to a young adult's concerns about phony, hypocritical Christians, assures them that all people are flawed. You will find time to share this with your young adult. We don't stop shopping at our favorite stores, eating at our favorite restaurants, or working with coworkers because people have issues. We don't attend church because everyone there is lovely, kind, and living right. To the contrary, church is the one place where we know people realize they are "sick"—sin sick. When we go to church, we understand we are all in the same boat—the boat that needs the Savior to rescue us and take us safely to where he wants us to go. Jesus himself said, "Those who are well have no need of a physician, but those who are sick ... For I did not come to call the righteous, but sinners, to repentance" (Matthew 9:12–13).

NEGATIVE CIRCUMSTANCES

Many young adults have been reared with the mindset that tried to protect them from disappointment or pain. For example, we thought we were doing our kids a favor by allowing every child to have a place on the team whether the child had talent for that sport or not. Then we took the mindset even further and gave every kid in the league a trophy, regardless of whether the team had won or lost games.

This thought process, which can be identified with the Self-Esteem Movement of the 1980s, entered schools when teachers received instructions to stop grading papers with red ink because this would damage the children's psyches. They were told to grade papers with green or purple or orange and give credit for effort by adding positive comments like "Great effort" or "I can tell you really tried hard." All of this ultimately led to the idea of social promotion, meaning students could not fail a grade for academic reasons, but would be passed on to the next grade to keep up socially with other kids in their age group.[2]

So now many millennials and Gen-Xers exist on false hope, having been lied to about their abilities. We failed to realize life would eventually teach them they can't do everything, win at everything, be the best at everything, and be the leader of everything. They would sometimes fail, come up short, and need help. We should have taught them Nelson Mandela's outlook: "I never lose; I either win or I learn."[3]

When confronted with negative circumstances—loss of a job, an accident, an illness, the death of a loved one—young adults are often totally blown away and decide to blame God.

A gentle response to the negative circumstance complaint involves identifying with the pain and loss your child is feeling. Take your time bringing God back into the conversation, as he shows himself to be the one on whom your child can still rely. God is fully capable of speaking up for himself in the love language that will draw your child back to him, and he may or may not use you in this process. Isn't it true we've learned some of our most enduring lessons through hardship and pain? It's difficult, but let God teach your son or daughter even if the lessons are taught using the textbook of suffering or a wilderness excursion.

NEED FOR A PERSONAL FAITH

Young adulthood is often a season of personal reflection. Whether they are in the military, college, or in their first real job, they may begin questioning many things about their family of origin, childhood, and previous experiences. Beliefs and practices they've accepted because parents and teachers relayed them, may now be subject to scrutiny. Your son or daughter may question not only what they believe, but also who they want to be for the rest of their lives. Since day one, everyone has tried to influence them to be something:

"Now be a big boy."
"You're such a big girl."
"You're not a scaredy-cat, are you?"
"Come on, join us!"
"Don't be like *them*."
"Everybody's trying it."
"Follow in your father's (or mother's) footsteps."
"Be your own man/woman."

Their departure from the faith might be a cry for self-realization—a desire to find their authentic self. The attempt to tear themselves away from God could be part of an experimental exercise in self-discovery. They will soon learn there is no place they can go where God is not. Psalm 139:7–10 sums this up:

Where can I go from Your Spirit? Or where can I flee from Your presence?
If I ascend into heaven, You *are* there;
If I make my bed in hell, behold, You *are there*.
If I take the wings of the morning,
And dwell in the uttermost parts of the sea,
Even there Your hand shall lead me,
And Your right hand shall hold me.

As my pastor, Rev. Welton Pleasant II, always tells us, "You will not know God is all you need until you get to the place where God is all you've got." When they need him, they'll discover God is still deep down inside.

If given the opportunity, share with your adult children stories from your times of doubt. What took you to those places? How did you find your way back to God? Be there for your young adults when they make the drastic decision they no longer believe in God and are leaving the faith. Know the salvation built upon their childhood declaration of faith in Jesus is just as binding in God's eyes as if they made that declaration when they were eighteen, or twenty-five, or thirty-five, or sixty. We cannot lose that which we didn't work to gain. Their verbal declaration can no more deny their salvation than they can change their DNA. Their DNA proves who their parents are no matter whether they want to be associated with them or not. Their spiritual DNA—Divine Nature Association—is more secure than a Gorilla Glue bond. Salvation forever associates them with the Divine, even as they pass through their discovery phase.

THE SWEET COMMUNION: HOW TO PRAY

Here is a prayer to get you started as you take your children to God over the issue of their desire to deny the faith. Fill in your son's or daughter's name below.

Dear God,

We know that your son, Jesus, has said he is the Way, the Truth, and the Life, and no one gets to you except through him. _____ has decided that to leave the faith because of no longer feeling the need for you or your son. We are really concerned about this because if _____ believes in Jesus, eternal life is the ultimate possession. If _____ does not obey Jesus, _____ will not see life, but your wrath will remain and _____ will not have life. (John 14:6, John 3:36, 1 John 5:11–12)

God, we know that _____ has been alienated from you and is behaving like an enemy in mind because of evil behavior and words against belief in you. We are asking that you show _____ that the reconciliation you have provided by what Christ did on the cross, rendering _____ without blemish and free from accusation. All _____ *must do is continue in the faith and not be moved from the hope held out in the gospel. (Colossians 1:21–23)*

Please shower your goodness, patience, and longsuffering onto _____ that will lead to repentance. It is not your will for _____ to die without turning back to you. (Romans 2:4, 2 Peter 3:9)

In Jesus's strong name, Amen.

THE SUPPORTIVE CONNECTIONS: WHERE TO TURN FOR ADDITIONAL HELP

Parents of young adults who have left the faith have many resources at their disposal. Start with the senior pastor, youth pastor, or young adult pastor of your local church. These people will be especially helpful if your child used to attend youth group activities and knows these leaders well. Have them reach out and perhaps invite your son or daughter to lunch or dinner so they can just talk and reestablish their friendship. The youth pastor may even have a place in the ministry where your child can assist with serving and even mentoring other young people. Rekindled involvement with an active youth ministry could very probably serve to help rekindle your child's involvement with the faith.

An adult Christian other than yourself, someone your young adult looks up to, is another option. You know how it is—you suggest, and your child thinks you're lame. But another person can make that same suggestion, and suddenly that's the best idea anyone has ever heard. Who is a part of your village who can come alongside you and continue to pour into your child's life?

Finally, research other churches (maybe even churches of different denominations than your own) or Christian parachurch organizations with active young adult ministries. Perhaps you can connect your adult child with community outreach work of some kind, and in the process, they may become friends with young adults in the program who also just happen to trust in Christ. Involvement in meaningful work together with other strong believers can be an opening for your son or daughter to see Christianity in action and making a difference. Jesus is lifted up when we do good works in his name, and he has promised that when he is lifted up, he will draw all people—including your child—to himself.

ARTICLES

"What the Self-Esteem Movement Got Disastrously Wrong" by Dan Sanchez. Foundation for Economic Education: FEE Stories. (May 15, 2017). https://fee.org/articles/what-the-self-esteem-movement-got-disastrously-wrong/.

"Christian Kids Are Leaving the Faith. What Can We Do About It?" by Catherine Segars Crosswalk.com Contributing Writer, February 9, 2022. https://www.crosswalk.com/family/parenting/christian-kids-leaving-the-faith-what-can-we-do.html

"UPDATED: Are Young People Really Leaving Christianity?" By J. Warner Wallace, Cold Case Christianity with J Warner and Jimmy Wallace. January 12, 2019, Updated October 30, 2021

BOOKS

Why Christian Kids Leave the Faith. By Tom Bisset. Discovery House Publishers, 1992.

Good News About Prodigals: Hope and Insight for Parents Who Wait for Their Child's Return. By Tom Bisset, 1998.

The Power of Praying® for Your Adult Children. By Stormie Omartian. Harvest House Publishers, 2014.

Hope Lies Ahead: Encouragement for Parents of Prodigals from a Family That's Been There. By James Banks and Geoffrey Banks. Our Daily Bread Publishing, 2020.

—CHAPTER 7—
I'M DROPPING OUT OF SCHOOL

THE SIMILAR CHRONICLES: YOU'RE NOT ALONE

ANTHONY'S STORY

Our first born and only son (we'll call him Xavier) dropped out of college after three semesters. Well, more accurately, poor performance and an incident in a dorm room with students smoking grass moved the university to say, "Sayonara!" Unfortunately, the setback did not initially serve as a kick in the pants for Xavier. I saw what no father wants to see—Xavier, my strong son, sat in a recliner for months, watching TV instead of interviewing for a job. His mother and I were upset at first, but we bit our tongues and watched to see what would happen with him. We guessed it might take a little time for him to figure himself out and remember who he was after being knocked down so hard.

After a while, Xavier became a fire fighter and then an ambulance driver. Next, he joined the Coast Guard where he began taking college courses to work his way to a degree. All was going well, and then, Uncle Sam stopped paying the GI Bill for education.

At the ripe age of thirty-six, ten years into his marriage and with a family of two, Xavier left the military but struggled to refind himself and a new career. Thankfully, he found himself again and graduated with straight As through an online college. Now, he's climbing the corporate ladder at a well-respected company and has begun an eighteen-month plan to gain his master's degree.

We gave him the space to do things his way, sent him a check for each college course once Uncle Sam stopped paying, and gave him emotional and financial support as he needed it. Xavier found his way in his own time. I believe it helped that he knew not only our values, but that we also had faith in God and in him.

THE STRESSFUL COMPLICATION: THE ISSUE/PROBLEM

The problem we face here lies not so much in the expectations of Scripture as it does in our personal expectations for our children. We pray over them as little ones and drill our expectations into their heads whether we realize we're doing it or not.

I was explicit about my expectations for my sons for higher education. From the time they were about five years old, we had regular conversations about what their young adult life would look like after they graduated from high school. I would tell them, "Now here's how life works: when you graduate from high school, you will go away to college. Although gaining a university education will require hard work, you'll have lots of fun living in the dorms, meeting new friends, exploring a new city, and being on your own making decisions as a grown-up." Every Thursday evening during their years as infants and toddlers, from 1987 through 1993, we delightedly watched *A Different World*, the mega-hit television show set at Hillman, the simulated historically Black university. My description of college as the kickoff of adult life and their enjoyment of this show made the decision to attend a university away from home a no-brainer.

Parents have solid and logical reasons for desiring their young adults get a college education. Post University, an accredited institution licensed by the state of Connecticut, published a blogpost on May 7, 2020, detailing "10 Great Reasons to Get your College Degree." Many of these reasons reflect the views we hold.

1. College helps you develop advanced writing skills. (As a retired English teacher, this might be my favorite reason, but I digress.)

2. You will develop newfound confidence as a public speaker. Meetings with employers, vendors, and team members on the job will require communication efficiency. Even in our technological age, we still must be able to verbally communicate effectively.

3. You will master the tech tools needed for success in today's economy.

4. Your college connections will help you build a professional network. The saying, "It's not what you know but who you know" is half true. Because you know the boss, doesn't mean you can effectively do the job. College provides both the connections and the know-how.

5. You'll discover exciting opportunities for advancement. You don't know what you don't know. Attending college opens vistas you had otherwise never heard of.

6. You will improve your lifelong earning potential. According to a key Georgetown University study entitled "The College Payoff," a bachelor's degree helps graduates earn on average 84 percent more over their lifetime than those who had only a high school diploma.

7. Your degree can shield you during times of high unemployment. In times of economic downturn,

employees without college degrees are often the first to lose their jobs.

8. You'll set a great example for your kids.

9. You may lead a longer, healthier life. According to a 2019 JAMA (Journal of the American Medical Association) study, those with four-year college degrees live longer than those with lesser levels of education.

10. You will feel a deep sense of personal satisfaction.[1]

Reasons 5–7 above were my main reasons for wanting my boys to go to college. I probably would not have been as cool and understanding as Xavier's parents if my boys had decided to skip or drop out of college. Yet and still, no matter how strong we feel our reasons may be, we must come to grips with the fact going to college is not a biblical mandate.

THE SAVIOR'S COMMUNICATION:
THE BIBLE'S MESSAGE

As much as we may wish it to be so, "Thou shalt get a college education," is not a verse in the Bible. We cannot point to anything in Scripture identifying skipping a university education as a sin. If our young adults decide not to pursue higher education, we cannot play the "God's going to get you if you don't" card.

We also cannot superimpose other Scripture upon what is strictly our child's personal choice. For example, the commandment to "honor your father and your mother" does not have anything to do with whether our children agree with our preferences of a life choice such as this (Exodus 20:12).

We may try to use Luke 9:62 where Jesus says, "No one, having put his hand to the plow, and looking back, is fit for the kingdom of God." Our argument might be crafted to explain how even Jesus himself says you shouldn't start something and then quit. The flaw in this argument is the fact Jesus is not talking about continuing a college education. He is discussing following him, which indeed can be done without a college education.

Without biblical back-up, what leg do we have to stand on when care-fronting our young adult who either refuses to enroll in college or drops out?

THE SINCERE CARE-FRONTATION

I am by no means saying we should give up on encouraging our children to get or continue with a college education. I am saying we engage in care-frontation when we offer a balanced view.

The first thing to realize is—and this is hard for me to admit as a life-long educator who loves school and believes in the learning process—college is not for everyone. (Ouch, tearing off the Band-Aid really, really hurt!) In fact, college is not even necessary to succeed at a high level in some professions. One gentleman I know, for example, spent his career working for the power company in several cities. His entry level position as a young man consisted of digging the holes for the power poles. As positions opened, he would participate in the on-the-job training and then advance to the new level. Each advancement added significant money to his paycheck. By the end of his career, his salary was well above many bachelor's degree holders his same age, and he had earned a retirement benefits package able to care for him the rest of his life.

Young people of every generation try to forge their own paths. This desire is natural in a young adult. Talking through as many of the alternatives as possible is a wise way to handle things when the subject of post-secondary education comes up. Here are some suggestions about broaching the topic:

1. Clarify this is an adult conversation. On this topic, make clear you are not operating as the sheriff in charge. You are owners of your home with the right to decide how people may and may not act in it. Your son or daughter is an adult with the right to make life decisions about school, and those decisions and subsequent actions may or may not line up with what you will tolerate from a person living in your home.

2. Listen to your child's reasons for not wanting to attend college. It may be a good idea to have him write them down so there will be no misunderstandings.

3. Now communicate your objections to any of those reasons. Do this in a calm way, the same way you allowed your child to talk to you.

4. Next, have your child enumerate the plans they have made. What will they do if they don't go to college? Is a job-hunting agenda in place? What kinds of jobs are they qualified for? Is the military a consideration? If so, which branch and what are the requirements? Does the plan include continuing living with you? If so, discuss the rent, the share of the household expenses and food, and your house rules (i.e., everyone in by midnight, all residents must go to church on Sunday, no members of the opposite sex spending the night, etc.—whatever your house rules may be).

5. Communicate clearly what you as parents can and are willing to do for your young adult. Life continues for both parents and kids once the kids are adults. Adults are responsible for themselves and are dysfunctional if they expect to be treated like adults but still act like children. Lodging, food, clothing, health care, utilities—none of these are free. Neither is recreation. It costs gas money to drive to the head

of the hiking trail, buy a movie ticket, or pay for the monthly Netflix service. Your son or daughter cannot have it both ways. (More about this in chapter 8).

Remember God allows us to be bruised, but still lets us move forward. There's nothing we can do about a lost opportunity. There is no gain in repeating, "I told you so," or rehearsing the errors. The mere fact the opportunity is gone is punishment enough. You are not excusing the mistake by letting it rest in the past. You are not canceling debts, or making excuses, or erasing the consequences. You are simply forgiving and moving forward within the present situation. Everything about who your child is still exists for you to love. Do your best to strike a balance between time to heal and catching fire anew. Allow a reasonable amount of time for redirection, then require your child to stand on his own two feet again. If that means going back to college, great. If it means going out into the world in a different, positive direction, that's great too.

THE SWEET COMMUNION: HOW TO PRAY

On the subject of post-secondary education, we want to pray for direction for our adult child. For each blank, fill in your child's name.

Dear God,

I would love for _____ to listen to what his father is saying and do exactly what his mother is teaching him. However, that is not the case right now as it relates to dropping out of college. So, I am asking you, Lord, to fill _____ with the wisdom you so generously give us when we ask you for it. Help _____ to realize childhood is over. It is time to start reasoning as an adult and give up childish ways. (Proverbs 6:20, James 1:5, 1 Corinthians 13:11)

I pray, dear God, you will direct _____'s

hands to find your will. Be it college, some other kind of employment, or the military, give _____ the excitement to do it with everything that's within. May _____ find passion to perform it heartily, as a service to you. (Ecclesiastes 9:10, Colossians 3:23) Bring _____ out of lethargy and depression over feelings of failure. Crush the urge to just be idle. Raise up in _____'s spirit the yearning to want to be busy and earn a satisfying living or give _____ a renewed zeal for school. Help _____ to finish what is started. Please God, communicate with _____ showing the right thing to do, allowing a vibrant conscience to remind of the truth that failing to do the right thing means is sin. Never allow _____ to be comfortable in sin.

Then, Lord, as _____ makes plans to either return to college or pursue some other Spirit-directed calling, give the stamina and the drive to be diligent, for your word promises the plans of the diligent will be blessed with abundance. (2 Thessalonians 3:7–13, James 4:17, Proverbs 21:5)

In Jesus's strong name, Amen.

THE SUPPORTIVE CONNECTIONS: WHERE TO TURN FOR ADDITIONAL HELP

My mother used to say, "There is more than one way to skin a cat." I never asked why my mother would know this, but I came to understand this saying means there are more paths to one goal than may be apparent at the time. This is indeed true of education. There are more ways to receive an education—even a college education—than starting college immediately after high school to push through the four or five years it will take to finish an undergraduate degree. Types of educational paths besides four-year universities include taking courses at community colleges and participating in online classes offered by accredited universities.

Other options for post-secondary education include internships or apprenticeships, which are on-the-job training opportunities. Young adults who are good with their hands may find their educational home at trade schools which exist to educate students in a particular field like auto mechanics, fashion design, construction, etc. Even personal mentors, trainers, and boot camps offer programs, easily discovered on the internet to teach people skills that can then be leveraged in the job market.

And do not underestimate the possibility of entrepreneurship. Many young people are striking out to make their visions reality by starting their own businesses. Of course, obtaining a university business degree couldn't hurt, but courses, books, and even YouTube videos exist to help us do just about anything. Who's to say your child is not the next Steve Jobs (co-founder of Apple), Bill Gates (co-creator of Microsoft), or Jeff Bezos (owner of Amazon. com)?

—CHAPTER 8—
I DON'T WANT TO WORK—ENTITLED, IRRESPONSIBLE, LAZY

THE SIMILAR CHRONICLES: YOU ARE NOT ALONE

CLOVINA'S STORY

Although my young adult children are not perfect, my nephew, my brother's oldest son, is the subject of this chapter. First, a little back story.

Our parents were good Baptist folks. Daddy was a deacon and mother did about everything else in the church. She sang in the choir, served on the usher board every fourth Sunday, cooked meals for church occasions, and taught VBS and Sunday school. Our pastor elevated her by licensing her as a minister and then ordaining her.

My brother, Dorian, and I were at church all the time. Our parents had us involved in children's and youth everything: choir, camp, cleaning crew, VBS, mission trips, etc. You name it, our names were on the roster.

The neat thing was, we both loved every minute of it. Our church friends were more important to us than our school friends. We grew up knowing church and knowing Jesus. We could both win any Bible Bowl game we entered.

We were all surprised then when Dorian married Zelda, who not only didn't come from our church but wasn't affiliated with any church. Zelda was a nice person, but she wasn't a Christian. When they started having kids, they didn't take them to church. Early on, they started having trouble with their oldest son. Because Dorian worked long hours, rearing the children was left to Zelda, and the strong-willed oldest one became too much for her to handle. When Dorian and Zelda divorced, the emotional toll on her meant the kids, then teenagers, were pretty much on their own to finish raising themselves.

Fast-forward to today. My dad died many years ago, and my brother passed away five years ago. I got married and moved out, so Mother lives alone. She can still care for her personal needs, but it's much more difficult to get around. Enter my brother's oldest son. He has moved himself in with his grandmother, but not to care for her. He is basically living off her. Her mortgage is paid, and her monthly social security and pension checks take care of her utilities and food bills. He's a thirty-five-year-old man living with her scot-free—no, sponging off her. He's eating food and using utilities, yet he's not cleaning up, not caring for the yard, not taking her to her doctors' appointments—nothing. He's her grandson, and neither she nor I can physically remove him.

In May of 2018, the story hit the news about parents Christina and Mark Rotondo, from Camillus, New York, a town west of Syracuse, who were forced to resort to legal action to remove their thirty-year-old son Michael from their home. He was not working nor was he contributing to the family in any way. Starting with discussions in October of 2017, his parents wrote notes to him about moving, and even offered monetary incentives, but Michael still refused to move. The case ended up in Judge Greenwood's court.[1]

This young man fought tooth-and-nail as his own attorney, arguing he had every right to stay in his parent's home, they were being unreasonable, and he should now be granted a six-month notice. After a lengthy argument with the judge, Greenwood grew tired of the son's disputing and ruled in favor of the parents. Michael intends to appeal. Amazing.

THE STRESSFUL COMPLICATION: THE ISSUE

The pressure is on for parents of young adults. These parents love their children and want to see them succeed in life. Graduation from high school and the eighteenth birthday are rites of passage launching these young folks into adulthood. Many parents expect to navigate this smoothly. The now-adult child will move on to an independent life. That, however, is not always the case. A report by the Pew Research Center has found a majority of young adults—52 percent—lived with one or both of their parents in July of 2020—a higher percentage than any previous measurement, including during the Great Depression.[2]

To add to the pressure, parents of eighteen- to twenty-four-year-olds are often also living in a sandwich situation. They find themselves approaching their retirement years, which they thought they'd be able to enjoy. Yet, they are not only dealing with their young adults, but are also serving as caregivers for their aging parents, many of whom are living into their nineties.

Some stressors on young adults have created pressures over which neither they nor we have control. These include a downturn in the economy, rising housing prices, soaring tuitions which have driven soaring student loan debt, and the cultural phenomena of delaying marriage.

As parents, we may have created our own problem of lazy, irresponsible, and entitled young adults in several ways. We've possibly spoiled them by never allowing them to feel the pain or suffer the consequences of any of their own poor choices.

For example, during my career as a high school English teacher, I would have one or two students each year who just blew off the importance of completing their homework. Of course, those students' grades began to drop, but they wanted to continue participating on their sports teams. When parents and coaches allowed those kids to stay on the team regardless of their grades, those kids failed to experience the consequences of their actions. Their negative behavior didn't teach them anything. Consequently, now as young adults, those kids do not expect to be held accountable and many continue to live without a sense of personal responsibility.

In our house, my youngest son, Mark, was an athlete, and his sport of choice was basketball. He played on teams from age five on. Twice he let his grades slide—once in middle school, and again as a freshman in high school. Both times, we pulled him off the team, not for just one game, but until the next report card. Both times, the coaches and other team members begged for him to be reinstated, pointing out he was a key player. That drew a hard no from us. Why? Mark had to learn he couldn't get what he wanted unless he fulfilled his responsibilities. The second benching hurt enough for Mark to catch on to this truth. He raised and maintained his grades, so he played throughout the rest of high school.

Another way we have created irresponsible kids is by not having a strong father figure in some homes, one who can lay down the law and put young adults out when this characteristic rears its ugly head. Too many households are run by parents who are simply afraid of their children. And again, this fear did not pop up overnight. When I suggested to one of my student's parents that she remove the television, video games, and computer from her child's room as a consequence for his behavior, she responded, "Then he'll be mad at me and slam the door in my face."

My counter response was, "In your house? Then you need to remove the door too. He obviously does not know how to operate a door properly, so he does not deserve to have one." Our first job is not to be our children's friends. They have friends—they need parents.

Children and adults are treated differently, and there will be different expectations from both sides as your children become adults. Even though young adults have certain expectations, the expectations that count the most are yours because you own the home. Before young adults move back in, set clear guidelines. For those who never moved out, communicate clearly childhood has ended, and adulthood has begun, therefore, new expectations are in place.

THE SAVIOR'S COMMUNICATION: THE BIBLE'S MESSAGE

God's position on laziness is clear—he is against it. Slothfulness is not a reflection of who God is, and by extension, it is not a reflection of what we should be like as a people who are to reflect God's character. In our introduction to God in Genesis chapter 1, we immediately come to know God as he is associated with work. He allows our first vision of him to be of a creator—he is working. And he works six days in a row before he rests. Then he rested not because he was tired, but because he was finished. We, too, are to work regularly until we finish the work God has planned for us to do.

Depending upon which version of the Bible you use, the idea of laziness is communicated using words like *slack*, *sluggard*, *slothful*, and *idle*. When dealing with a lazy young adult, we must realize we can stake our position, and thus our ultimatums, firmly on the word of God without guilt or regret.

The Bible describes a lazy person as one who destroys. The sluggard has desires but won't work so gets nothing and is ultimately considered to be denying the faith which makes him worse than an unbeliever.

- "He who is slothful in his work is a brother to him who is a great destroyer" (Proverbs 18:9).
- "The soul of a lazy *man* desires, and *has* nothing; but the soul of the diligent shall be made rich" (Proverbs 13:4).
- "But if anyone does not provide for his own, and especially for those of his household, he has denied the faith and is worse than an unbeliever" (1 Timothy 5:8).

According to Scripture, some of the results of laziness and irresponsibility include the house falling in, poverty, and bringing shame to the family. In other words, big problems will occur because little things are neglected. For example, if a person does not do something as simple as brush his teeth every day, he will end up with cavities, gum disease, and tooth loss. Or if your young adult refuses to clean up, an insect infestation could occur, resulting in a large bill for extermination.

- "Because of laziness the building decays, And through idleness of hands the house leaks" (Ecclesiastes 10:18).
- "How long will you slumber, O sluggard? When will you rise from your sleep? A little sleep, a little slumber, A little folding of the hands to sleep—so shall your poverty come on you like a prowler, and your need like an armed man" (Proverbs 6:9–11).
- "He who has a slack hand becomes poor, but the hand of the diligent makes rich. He who gathers in summer is a wise son; he who sleeps in harvest is a son who causes shame" (Proverbs 10:4–5).

Our response to the lazy, irresponsible person should mirror God's response. His word says a person who won't work, shouldn't eat. In other words, people who are able yet refuse to pull their own weight should be left to their own devices regarding their care. Parents need not feel responsible for children who are perfectly capable of being responsible for themselves. Rather than catering to and caring for them, parents should encourage and command them to earn their own living.

- "For even when we were with you, we commanded you this: If anyone will not work, neither shall he eat. For we hear that there are some who walk among you in a disorderly manner, not working at all, but are busybodies. Now those who are such we command and exhort through our Lord Jesus Christ that they work in quietness and eat their own bread" (2 Thessalonians 3:10–12).

Instead of being lazy, irresponsible, and unresourceful, God's intention for his children is quite inspiring. Ephesians 2:10 tells us we are "his workmanship"—specifically from Greek, we are God's *poema*, his poem, creatively drafted and crafted by God's hands in Christ Jesus. He made us for a purpose—good works. What? Yes, God intended for us, all of us including our adult children, to participate in good works he has "prepared beforehand" for us to do.

Let's allow God's word to wrap up this section about the Bible's message related to laziness. "See then that you walk circumspectly, not as fools but as wise, redeeming the time, because the days are evil. Therefore do not be unwise, but understand what the will of the Lord *is*" (Ephesians 5:15–17).

THE SINCERE CARE-FRONTATION

How do you care for and confront your young adult son or daughter who refuses to work? In my parenting book,

Boomerangs to Arrows: A Godly Guide for Launching Young Adult Children, or what I jokingly suggest should have been entitled *How to Get Your Grown Kids Out of Your House,* I submit God intended for parents to raise their children with the understanding they will become independent adults. When God said a man is blessed when his quiver is full of children, he was giving parents a strong hint. Quivers are full of arrows, not boomerangs. Parents are to aim children and send them off into successful adult lives away from the family home.[3]

Parental aiming, along with realizing how precious and fleeting our time is with our children, takes place in *Just 18 Summers,* as Michele Cox and Rene Gutteridge point out in their book by the same name.[4]

This chapter is not intended to take parents to task just because adult children live at home. There are as many reasons for this arrangement as there are families in which it happens. This chapter is specifically addressing parenting young adults who refuse to pull their own weight no matter where they live. The characteristics of laziness, entitlement, and irresponsibility are at issue here.

Now is not too late for you to insist your children accept the responsibilities of adulthood. You pay the rent or mortgage on your home, so you have the right to say what happens in it and who lives there. Plan a formal meeting with your children at which you will have a heart-to-heart talk with them. Affirm your love for them, then discuss the problem as you see it. Read from your prepared statement what you have to say to them. To combat laziness, tell them what they need to do to continue living under your roof. Be specific. Your requests are nonnegotiable. Here are some conditions other parents have required, including having their young adult sign a contract agreeing to the following:

- Set a date for moving out

- Obey house rules like no smoking, no overnight guests, in the house for the night by a certain hour, attending church, etc.

- Submit a percentage of their paycheck to the parent in trust for future moving expenses

- Maintain clean living quarters (her room, bathroom, closet, etc.)

- Share in general housework inside and out

- Negotiate the use of shared spaces

- Share in utility bills or risk losing their use

- Pay personal bills such as cell phone, car note, gas, health and car insurances, clothing, cleaning, personal hygiene items, internet, cable or satellite services, entertainment, etc.

If you fear your children, get assistance before talking with them about your new requirements. Either move the meeting to a different location or have others present during the meeting. If you do not have relatives who can maintain their composure, have some of the men from your church attend the meeting, not to participate, but just to have your back. Hopefully, it will never come to this, but if your fear is such you think your children might physically harm you, you need to get the police involved. Tell your children how you expect things to change and then obtain a restraining order if necessary.

THE SWEET COMMUNION: HOW TO PRAY

Dear God,

I am bringing _____ to you today because of laziness and irresponsibility. Your word clearly states _____ will end up in poverty without getting it together, getting up, and getting to work. I need your help to motivate _____. (Proverbs

10:4, 20:13)

Lord, I realize laziness and irresponsibility will lead _____ into hunger, shame, and forced labor. _____'s laziness is ultimately sin. Please forgive _____and provide an awakening in order for them to realize the sin is ultimately against you. (Proverbs 19:15; 12:24; 10:5; James 4:17)

I ask you continue to be patient with _____ until such time as responsibility becomes a lifestyle. I turn my child over to you to use whatever means necessary to move _____ to that place. Strengthen me to be able to put my foot down in whatever way is necessary to agree with your plan for _____'s adult life. May your goodness lead to _____'s repentance before your discipline must do it. (2 Peter 3:9, Romans 2:4, Hebrews 12:11)

I look forward to the day when _____ is operating as a successful, independent adult. You will get all the glory!

In Jesus's strong name, Amen.

THE SUPPORTIVE CONNECTIONS: WHERE TO TURN FOR ADDITIONAL HELP

PERSONAL FAMILY MEMBERS.

Perhaps grandparents, an uncle, or an aunt could reason with your child about taking on adult responsibilities. This should be a person your adult child admires, respects, and would not want to disappoint.

TURN TO YOUR LOCAL CHURCH.

This is the work of pastors, to help their parishioners grow and mature as believers. Your pastor could possibly have a conversation with your adult child, not as the Sunday school kid, but as the now-adult who is stepping into an independent future.

CHRISTIAN COUNSELING.

Securing a mentor or life coach is a popular approach. Engaging such a person takes the onus off you as the bad guy who wants to kick your child out of the house and places the focus on the young adult to be empowered to move forward. Several resources I found are:

The Christian Counselor Directory—The great thing about the counselors listed here is the variety of ways they can be contacted to discuss your sensitive issues. This site suggests you can "contact our therapists about virtual sessions, including video, phone, chat, or other method during this challenging time." https://www.christiancounselordirectory.com/

Faithful Counseling--Here you can connect with a fellow believer online within their network of licensed, professional therapists. https://www.faithfulcounseling.com/

Find Christian Counselor at http://www.findchristiancounselor.com. They say, "The Christian therapists in our network provide individual, marriage, and family counseling." You fill out the simple form online and then you will be directed to the therapist closest to your location.

—CHAPTER 9—
I ABUSE DRUGS/ALCOHOL

THE SIMILAR CHRONICLES: YOU ARE NOT ALONE

CECILY'S STORY

A letter in my oldest son's handwriting lay on the kitchen table. My mind flashed to the numerous letters he had written me as I looked at the quickly jotted scribble of his name on the wrinkled paper. This was the son we had prayed over in my womb. "The baby's trapped in your left fallopian tube," the doctor said. "You will need surgery, Mrs. Smith, or you will lose the baby."

My husband and I walked out of the doctor's office thinking *God's will be done*. I was only sixteen, married to a US Army soldier who was due to deploy any day. What were we thinking to start a family so young? We prayed for God's will. Then I felt a pop in my belly—that's right, a literal "pop." The next exam showed a growing fetus in my womb, right where the baby was supposed to be. Months later, after a normal delivery, William Luke III was born, a strong boy with Christian parents bolstered by a strong faith in a God who had done the miraculous.

Will decided to surrender his life to Jesus at an early age. By the time he was sixteen, he knew he wanted to enter the military, following in his dad's footsteps. The Marine Corps was no joke, so to our knees we fell, praying for God to protect him. Will graduated at the top of his class and began a promising military career. How proud we were to watch our godly son walk across the courtyard at graduation.

Maybe the Marine Corps was too tough, or maybe the influence of all the other guys became too strong. Whatever the reason, alcohol entered Will's life and started to steal the son we knew little by little, day by day. The number of those great letters he used to send began to decline. He even stopped calling and the chasm between us widened.

After Will left the Marine Corps, the demon of alcohol escorted him in and out of numerous rehabs. We endured months of silence, then we'd get letters from jail, then more silence, then late-night phone calls, and so on. This pattern droned on for years.

The letter on the kitchen table appeared after a more than twenty-year estrangement. I was on my way to minister on a Christian cruise. My son had possibly dropped by while driving on a suspended driver's license. I opened the letter and four dollars fell to the table. The letter said:

Dear Mom, I am so sorry for the failure I have been. I know I have caused you so much pain over the years. I promise to try to do better. Here is 4 dollars so you can buy you a soda or something on your trip.

I suppose I should have been touched, but my tears for this boy were all dried up. Will's letters always said the same thing, and the promises never played out. I never knew when I would get the call he had died somehow.

I still wait. Will is in his forties now. I still pray and have faith he will be all right. He attends church sometimes, works sometimes, and we see him sometimes. I held on to those four dollars, praying for the day I could spend them with him to celebrate moving forward in his life.

When I returned from the cruise, Will called, and wanted to spend some time with me. We went to the movies, and I spent the four dollars with him. We had a fun day, and we kept the conversation light. I continue to believe God will "pop" Will out of the trap of alcoholism just like he popped out the baby trapped in my fallopian tube, and our prodigal son will return home. I cling to the verse from Proverbs 22:6 because we have "train[ed] up [our son] in the way he should go" and we're just waiting to see the manifestation of the promise "when he is old, he will not depart from it." God loves us, and he still loves Will. I believe we will get to spend another four dollars on a soda together.

EVELYN'S STORY:

I was beyond excited when my daughter called me at work to say she was in labor. She had been scheduled for a Cesarean procedure two weeks later so she could avoid labor, but her little guy and the Lord decided now was the time for his debut. My daughter was single, so I was on deck to be in the delivery room with her. As soon as I arrived at the hospital, the staff was waiting to get me scrubbed and gowned. Surgery was still necessary, but it went well. I was escorted into the nursery where I sat in a rocking chair, stroked my grandson's face, and sang to him. Two days later, my daughter returned home without the baby. Child Protective Services (CPS) had taken him and placed him in foster care. He had tested positive for meth.

I was furious. My daughter told me she had only used once, but everybody knows everything the mother takes in filters to the baby through the umbilical cord. What was she thinking? Clearly, she wasn't thinking. Where had I gone wrong to raise a child who would make such a ridiculous, dangerous choice? Had she not paid attention at all in the many years we had spent together in church?

We had to be in court three days after she was discharged from the hospital. The judge asked if I was willing to take custody of the baby. Of course, I was, but it still took four and a half months to get him out of the foster care system. I attended numerous court hearings and was interviewed intensively. CPS representatives went to my apartment to see if it was suitable. I had to make modifications to the cabinets and buy a fire extinguisher.

The good news is my daughter entered a Christian-based residential treatment program for two years. I could take my grandson to visit her. All we could hope was once authorities saw she was making progress; the court would return her custody rights.

THE STRESSFUL COMPLICATION: THE ISSUE

Alcoholic beverages seem to have been around throughout recorded history. According to the National Center for Biotechnology Information and other corroborating resources, proof of the use of alcoholic beverages can be traced as far back as 7000 BC.[1] Throughout history, alcohol consumption accompanied feasts and celebrations of all kinds. No wonder by the time the Bible was written, God instructed his writers to warn us of the evils of intoxication. The biblical writers used the word *pharmakeia,* and *The King James Bible Dictionary* lists Thayer's definition as "the use or the administering of drugs (like medication), poisoning, sorcery, magical arts."[2] The word is also found in connection with idolatry.

Fast forward to the nineteenth century and we find the temperance and prohibition movements, which eventually caused the United States to pass laws severely restricting "the manufacture, sale, import and export of intoxicating liquors." But despite the restrictions, the money in the booming alcohol trade caused those laws to be overturned and prohibition was canceled. Now "an estimated 15 million Americans suffer from alcoholism and 40% of all car accident deaths in the US involve alcohol."[3]

Few people would argue about the dangers of drug and alcohol abuse, so why is it still such a huge problem? The answer is easy. Like anything else proven bad for us, our freedom to choose mingled with our free will acts as a mixed drink laced with drugs affecting our decision-making abilities. We overestimate our ability to hold our liquor or handle the hit. When something is not illegal yet injurious—like smoking cigarettes, using marijuana, and drinking alcoholic beverages—we must be even more watchful than when we are facing other types of choices.

My mother lived as a perfect example of what some of us may have to do regarding our relationship with alcohol. One day, I noticed she didn't drink wine or any kind of liquor, so I asked her why. She said, "I tried wine once and I liked it, so that's why I don't drink it." At first her comment confused me. Then she explained she had seen the negative effects of alcoholism in other people's lives, and she vowed never to end up like them. She's sure they didn't start out with the plan to become addicted. By liking the taste, she realized she could easily drink more and more and succumb to an alcoholic's fate, so she made the choice not to drink wine at all. Wise woman.

THE SAVIOR'S COMMUNICATION: THE BIBLE'S MESSAGE

Although Jesus's first miracle sees him operating as a vintner (winemaker), his actions do not endorse the overuse of intoxicating drinks. God intends for us to understand his Word and most issues are explained quite clearly. We don't need to apply a lot of Scriptural gymnastics to comprehend God's will about being controlled by alcohol or drugs.

The pastor of a church I attended used to teach us about Scripture exegesis. He would say, "When plain sense makes good sense, seek no other sense." The King James Version's rendering of Ephesians 5:18 says, "And be not drunk with wine, wherein is excess; but be filled with the Spirit." Pretty clear, right? Other translations and paraphrases further clarify the word "excess" to say getting drunk will ruin your life, cheapens your life, and is a form of rebellion. Other verses go on to explain the many evils lying along the path of the person who is overcome by alcohol, and its overuse destroys the partakers, rendering them wicked, corrupt, and even stupid.

But perhaps reading Ephesians 5:18 alone does not make a convincing enough argument against substance abuse. In this case, try these cross references from the English Standard Version:

> Wine is a mocker, strong drink a brawler, and whoever is led astray by it is not wise. (Proverbs 20:1)

> Nor thieves, nor the greedy, nor drunkards, nor revilers, nor swindlers will inherit the kingdom of God. (1 Corinthians 6:10)

> Now the works of the flesh are evident, which are: adultery, fornication, uncleanness, lewdness, idolatry, sorcery [Greek *pharmakeia* = drug abuse], hatred, contentions, jealousies, outbursts of wrath, selfish ambitions, dissensions, heresies, envy, murders, drunkenness [Greek *methe* = intoxication], revelries, and the like; of which I tell you beforehand, just as I also told *you* in time past, that those who practice such things will not inherit the kingdom of God. (Galatians 5:19–21)

> The older women likewise, that they be reverent in behavior, not slanderers, not given to much wine, teachers of good things. (Titus 2:3)

THE SINCERE CARE-FRONTATION

Caring for our young adult son or daughter who is tending toward alcoholism or addiction requires our involvement rather than our detachment, at least at first. Action is better than inaction. Let the withdrawal of our involvement become a last-ditch effort to apply pressure which may lead to change.

The critical importance of doing everything we can to convince the child to turn from alcohol and drug use lies in the Greek word *pharmakeia* as discussed above. The unearthly hold exerted by addictive substances seems to be backed by other-worldly sources. In other words, the grasp upon one's life could be a Satanic stronghold. We must do our best to remember: "We do not wrestle against flesh and blood, but against principalities, against powers, against the rulers of the darkness of this age, against spiritual hosts of wickedness in the heavenly places" (Ephesians 6:12). It is worth the battle to fight Satan for our young adults.

My research led me to the same best practice when trying to convince someone to stop drinking or using. The best approach is open communication. Neither broaching the subject nor not keeping the conversation going may be easy, but the effort is worth it. Alcohol and drug use produce a physical dependence, which, when added to the Satanic stronghold, makes this a tough habit to break. Addictions do not start in one day, so they probably will not end in one day either. Most victims need the aid of professionals or at least empathetic friends or family.

Contrary to popular opinion, every alcoholic or addict does not have to hit rock bottom before quitting. God can intervene early in the addictive process. We tend to give up on people because we're frustrated, not because they are beyond hope.

People can also quit immediately when the right argument is made. For example, after being a two-pack-a-day smoker for many years, my husband quit instantly when he heard the United States surgeon general discuss how the warning on the pack had been changed. From 1966 to 1970, warning labels said, "Caution: Cigarette smoking may be hazardous to your health." Then from late 1970 to

1985, new warning labels said, "Warning: The surgeon general has determined cigarette smoking is dangerous to your health." My husband quit in 1985 when he saw the report and read the new labels with their painfully specific statement: "Surgeon General's Warning: Smoking causes lung cancer, heart disease, emphysema, and may complicate pregnancy." He looked at the package and said, "Well then, I'm a darn fool," and he has not smoked another cigarette since that day.[4]

Even with such examples and explicit warning, many people are not moved to quit smoking. SoberServices.com lists six other ways to convince an alcoholic or addict to accept help.

1. Use Sober Intervention—Considered by this site to be the most effective, loving, and healthy way to confront the alcoholic or addict, the family gets together to confront the young adult's behaviors with absolute love, complete honesty, and strong bottom-line boundaries.

2. Use Social Proof Intervention—Engage the young adult in conversation with someone who has already recovered and is well into the journey of recovery.

3. Use the Services of a Sober Professional or a Former Alcoholic/Addict—Hearing from a professional—the surgeon general—was the technique which moved my husband to quit smoking.

4. Find Out the Reasons Why the Person Won't Get Help

5. Determine the Solutions (to the reasons why the person won't get help)

6. Talk to Them instead of Talking at Them[5]

Alcohol and drug abuse are often accompanied by other problems detrimental not only to the alcohol and drug abusers but also to those around them. This cannot be allowed and should not be tolerated under any circumstances. In such cases, you have every right to feel no guilt about removing yourself and other family members from harm's way or taking necessary steps to remove that person from your presence.

THE SWEET COMMUNION: HOW TO PRAY

As hard as it may be, our prayers must be focused away from the problem and onto the solution found in Christ alone. To get started on this new prayer focus, here is a prayer based upon Scriptures dealing with addictive behavior. By praying God's Word back to him, you can be assured you are praying his will right on target for your child. Fill your young adult's name in the blanks.

Dear God,

You are my rock and my deliverer. I am welcomed to run to you when I need help. I really need you to stabilize and deliver me from the worry I am experiencing over the alcoholism/drug use of my (son/daughter) _____. I need you, God, to be _____'s rock and _____'s deliverer right now too.

You are also my shield and stronghold. I need you to shield me from Satan's attacks as he taunts me to think I will lose my child to this addiction. Help me grow strong in faith. Please also be _____'s shield too. Until _____ is free from addiction, shield my child from danger when my child is drunk or high, and keep _____ away from drugs laced with even stronger substances that could immediately take my child's life. (Psalm 18:2–6)

I pray, God, you would completely take the taste for liquor out of _____'s mouth. Block the supplier of the drugs. Convince _____ that being led away by wine, strong drink, and drugs is not wise. Also take people out of _____ *'s life who participate in drinking and/or doing drugs. If those friends stay, please deliver them from their addictive behaviors as well.* (Proverbs 20:1; 1 Corinthians 15:33)

This prayer is offered to you, Lord, in faith because I trust how your Word says the prayer of faith will save the sick. _____ *is sick within this addiction. Change* _____ *'s entire motivation so there will no longer be a craving for strong drink or drugs. Turn my child's life around so* _____ *will desire being controlled by your Spirit.* (James 5:15–16; Ephesians 5:18)

In Jesus's mighty name, Amen.

THE SUPPORTIVE CONNECTIONS: WHERE TO TURN FOR ADDITIONAL HELP

Be encouraged because many resources are available to both the alcoholic or drug abuser and those who want to help them. Many churches and community organizations host groups to help. Alcoholics Anonymous is probably the most well-known program, but others can be effective as well. On the internet, search for "help for alcoholism" or "help for drug addiction." You will also be able of to search for meetings close to you in addition to being able to surf through the websites of all the organizations you find.

Two national groups include:

Alcoholics Anonymous—https://www.aa.org/

American Addictions Centers—https://www.alcohol.org/advocacy-groups/

—CHAPTER 10—
I'M IN TROUBLE WITH THE LAW

THE SIMILAR CHRONICLES: YOU ARE NOT ALONE

GREGORY'S STORY

Nobody wants to get *that* call.

"Hi, Dad. I need you to come down to the police department. I've been arrested and I need you to bail me out. Please."

I did the best I could being a father to Amadi. After his mother and I broke up, and she got custody of Amadi, she, her new boyfriend, and his daughter moved a hundred miles away from where I lived. The distance and my work schedule conspired to make it difficult for me to see Amadi regularly and exert my values upon him. When we were together on the weekends, I would take him to church with me, and he seemed to really like it. We would talk about serious topics like education, drugs, and sex, but I didn't want to spend all my precious time with him being heavy. We wanted to have fun together, too, so went to basketball and baseball games and played video games together.

Then one day, while playing with his stepsister, Amadi had the bright idea to play Blowtorch: a stupid game where you light a match, then blow the flame. Well, his stepsister suffered a burn on her face, her dad called the cops, and at fourteen, Amadi was taken from his mother. Instead of the system letting me have custody, they placed him in a group home for four years. In that environment, he had to learn how to survive. So, he spent his formative years, from fourteen to eighteen, learning to be mean to get his way.

Amadi was released from the group home when he turned eighteen, but it didn't take long before I began getting *that* call. He didn't know how to function in relationships and would get rough with his girlfriends. They'd call the police, he'd get arrested, and the cycle kept going. Because of his growing record, he found it difficult to get steady work, and he became depressed. His depression led him to self-medicate, and of course, drug use eventually leads either to prison or death. Prison was the destination for Amadi.

THE STRESSFUL COMPLICATION: THE ISSUE

All the Christian parents I know do their best to help their children distinguish right from wrong. At home with their children, as well as in community with extended family members, teachers, Sunday school instructors, and others, parents depend upon their village to help them communicate godly values. Every lesson builds upon the last, and no lesson is too small. We hope the cumulative effort of every teaching opportunity leads our children to internalize moral values that not only will keep them out of prison but will also make them productive members of society.

Thus was the case with what is now one of our family's favorite teachable moments. For two years, my sons Matthew and Mark attended the high school where I taught. Thus, they stayed after school with me while I graded papers and prepared for the following day. Matthew usually used the time to get his homework done. Mark, on the other hand, spent his energy playing basketball with his friends.

One afternoon, the afterschool program coordinator bought pizza for the kids in her care. She left the boxes in the teachers' lounge while she went to her classroom to work with her charges. Matthew and Mark were not in the program; however, Mark found out about the pizza and decided to commandeer it for himself and his basketball buddies. Okay, he stole it. He and his friends had a grand time causing the pie to quickly disappear. When the program coordinator discovered the pizza was missing, of course, no one knew anything about what happened to it. About the same time, I exited my classroom and was made aware of the disappearing pizza mystery. I asked Matthew and Mark if they knew anything about it, and they both said no. We drove home.

The next morning at school, the heat was turned up and the inquiry continued to find the pizza thieves. Eventually, Mark's friends sang, and now I had to step in. I was livid and embarrassed to learn my son was the guilty party who had stolen the pizza and then lied about it. This boy was a good sized fifteen-year-old, past the spanking age, but obviously not past his mischievous antics.

"So, you are a thief and a liar now?" I queried. "God tells me to train you according to your bent, so since you are bent on being a thief, I know you are going to end up in prison. You are going to have to learn how to be a prisoner. First, give me those nice Nikes. Prisoners don't wear designer shoes." I piled both of my boys into the car and headed for the discount shoe store. "You'll need plain shoes with Velcro closures because you might want to hang yourself with your shoelaces." Mark immediately had to start wearing those ugly shoes.

Next, we headed to the discount clothing store. "Prisoners don't wear name brand name slacks and shirts either." I bought him a plain white button-up shirt and plain blue unstructured pants. "You will wear these every day and wash them every night." He wasn't happy.

Then we drove to the barbershop. Mark had been wearing neat braids he and the girls loved. "Now the braids come off." We all got out of the car, but he refused to go into the shop. For the first time in his life, he openly defied me. Teenagers can be stubborn, but he had never pushed me to my limits, and he was about to find out just how determined this Black woman was to teach this lesson and win this battle.

I told Matthew to get back into the car, and I drove away, leaving Mark standing in front of the barbershop. I drove around to the back of the building and called their stepdad. I started, "Honey, you are going to have to tell me what to do because I am about to get arrested for child endangerment." After I ran down the rest of the story of the afternoon to him, he said, "Bring him home."

I went back and picked Mark up. No words were exchanged, but when we pulled into the driveway, Pop came out of the back door, and Mark took off running. He called his brother to check in and communicated his demands through Matthew. Obviously, Mark was unclear of his position. He would be allowed to come home when he submitted to our demands for obedience.

Mark stayed away for the rest of the night; however, he showed up at school later the next day wearing the clothes and shoes I had bought him and with his homework done. He avoided me around campus all day but apologized after school and asked to come home. I said he could, but we headed to the barbershop first. He emerged with a very low haircut and then, of course, had to face Pop's punishment as well. Except for school, Mark was "imprisoned" at home for the next two to three weeks. He wore those clothes, too, but he did draw a Nike swoosh on the shoes.

At the writing of this book, Mark is now in his thirties. He has never been in prison. In fact, he graduated from high school and college, got married, has three kids, and has no need to steal anything because, with his wife, he supports his family as the self-employed entrepreneur of their extremely successful pool cleaning service.

I will never forget the embarrassment and feelings of failure I felt upon discovering my child was the guilty pizza thief. I can only imagine those same feelings being magnified when your adult child commits an offense and lands in jail. You don't participate in the conversations about what everyone's grown children are up to. People know there must be a problem if you suddenly stop talking about your kid, so the shame mounts. Others can guess your child is in prison if your child is not away at college or the military.

As with Mark's pilfering escapade, we must be careful not to condone a criminal disposition we see blossoming in our children. Call it out and nip it in the bud. Once our kids are young adults living on their own, we may want to overlook what we see as "minor" crimes because they may even benefit us. By accepting money or gifts you know have been gained through illegal means, you are aiding and abetting the criminal activity and could also be held liable.

THE SAVIOR'S COMMUNICATION: THE BIBLE'S MESSAGE

When one of the Pharisees asked Jesus to tell him which was the foremost commandment, Jesus did not answer the man using one of the Big Ten found in Exodus chapter 20. He quoted the second phrase of the *Shema* found in Deuteronomy 6:5, "You shall love the LORD your God with all your heart, with all your soul, and with all your strength." (Compare this with Matthew 22:37, Mark 12:30, and Luke 10:27.) Jesus also quoted Leviticus 19:18, adding that this second commandment was just as important as the first: "You shall love your neighbor as yourself."

The point is: If we love God and love our neighbor, we will act accordingly and live in a world free of sinning against one another. In the context of our current discussion, if we love God and love our neighbors, we will not do anything to them or against them to cause us to be on the wrong side of the law. We will not do anything worthy of being arrested, and we won't end up in jail.

Ezra 7:26 clearly expresses God's view about what should happen when we don't act in a loving manner toward others and break the law. "Whoever will not observe the law of your God and the law of the king, let judgment be executed speedily on him, whether *it be* death, or banishment, or confiscation of goods, or imprisonment." Deuteronomy 21:18–21 expresses how serious God is about children— even grown children—obeying their parents:

> If a man has a stubborn and rebellious son who will not obey the voice of his father or the voice of his mother, and *who* when they have chastened him, will not heed them, then his father and his mother shall take hold of him and bring him out to the elders of his city, to the gate of his city. And they shall say to the elders of his city, 'This son of ours is stubborn and rebellious; he will not obey our voice; he is a glutton and a drunkard.' Then all the men of his city shall stone him to death with stones; so you shall put away the evil from among you, and all Israel shall hear and fear.

Parents are responsible to teach children the difference between right and wrong. In fact, Ecclesiastes 8:11 tells us, "Because the sentence against an evil work is not executed speedily, therefore the heart of the sons of men is fully set in them to do evil." It's important for parents to do their job early.

The book of Proverbs is another place where we find instruction on raising children to have a moral compass.

Solomon wrote these wise sayings, not as commandments or promises, but as practical guidelines. Each one should be read as if it were telling us if we operate in this particular way, we should experience this particular outcome. Proverbs 22:6 tells parents to "train up a child in the way he should go" and suggests "when he is old, he will not depart from" the training. Fathers are given additional instruction about raising their kids in Ephesians 6:4 where they are told, "Fathers, do not provoke your children to wrath, but bring them up in the training and admonition of the Lord."

Children have responsibilities too. Ephesians 6:1–3 tells them, "Children, obey your parents in the Lord, for this is right. Honor your father and mother, which is the first commandment with promise: 'that it may be well with you and you may live long on the earth.'"

When young adult children decide to go their way and get in trouble with the law, they will suffer consequences. Deuteronomy 24:16 states, "Fathers shall not be put to death for *their* children, nor shall children be put to death for *their* fathers; a person shall be put to death for his own sin." If those children end up in prison, their parents ought not detest and disown them. Despite their embarrassment and disappointment, parents (and indeed the rest of us) are to extend empathy. Hebrews 13:3 tells us, "Remember the prisoners as if chained with them—those who are mistreated—since you yourselves are in the body also."

THE SINCERE CARE-FRONTATION

How do we care for and confront our young adults who are in trouble with the law? To answer this question, I combined my suggestions with information from websites like the one from the Department of Justice, which discuss how to best treat inmates to reduce the recidivism rate.

Care-frontation begins with keeping every possible line of communication open between us and our troubled grown kids. One dad I know just couldn't bear visiting his son in prison because of all he had to go through just to get in to see him. The father told me he was patted down upon entering the facility and was then ushered through several doors, which were slammed and locked behind him. The horror of the experience was a strong motivator for his son to change his ways once he was released so as not to have to ask his father to go through such degradation again.

Visits are still at the top of the communication list, if possible. Nothing replaces seeing one another face-to-face. Sometimes, especially in the event of federal prison placements, visits are not possible because the distance is great and expensive. If visits are out, go for the next best thing—telephone calls.

Next, write letters. Having letters delivered tells your child they are being thought about—not out of sight and out of mind. Work as a family to be sure regular communication is received. Perhaps Mom could write a letter every Monday, Dad could write on Tuesday, Sister on Wednesday, Brother on Thursday, Grandma on Friday, and Granddad on Saturday. You don't have to write a whole letter every time. Sometimes you could use your day to send a postcard or a greeting card.

There is also email. Some prisons have an electronic mail system through which you can communicate with your inmate. The loss of privacy is part of the punishment of incarceration, so the messages are checked to be sure nothing illegal is being communicated; however, so are your other letters. This is yet another way to keep in touch.

The American prison system is designed more for punishment than for rehabilitation, so your voice may be the voice of therapy. Now your son or daughter is locked up with lots of empty time on their hands, they may feel more open to hearing you and speaking the truth about their actions and responsibilities. Are you able to tell the truth in an understanding way? Are you able to listen effectively and allow them to talk their way to understanding themselves and their motivations?

To prevent recidivism, starting with the first day of incarceration, gather information about your child's risk of relapsing and develop an individualized plan for reentry. According to the Department of Justice, inmates who participate in correctional education programs have 43 percent lower odds of returning to prison, so encourage your child to develop marketable job skills. If necessary, ensure your young adult receives appropriate substance abuse treatment and prioritize mental health treatment.

With all this consistent attention and assistance, your child's time may be reduced for good behavior, or at least their prison time may be less stressful. As release approaches, do your best to equip your inmate with information and resources to prepare to return to the community. Help them maintain government-issue ID's. Without these, they will face extreme challenges securing employment, registering for school, opening bank accounts, accessing health benefits, and so on, all of which are critical to his successful return to the community.[1]

THE SWEET COMMUNION: HOW TO PRAY

The Bible discusses what our attitude toward prisoners should be. If the person in prison is our adult child, we are not excused from God's intentions. We can tell God our frustrations and embarrassments, but we still must break through those hurts to lift our children to the Father while they are in trouble with the law.

Dear God,

I am so frustrated with _____. I am worried about _____ and am not sure what to do to

help. Please guide me and protect _____.
I really tried to raise _____ in the way you said
children should go—following you to show me what
you had built _____ to be. Sometimes it doesn't
look like _____ will turn to you, but I'm trusting
you will be the draw. (Proverbs 22:6)

Your word does not have good things to say about
a stubborn and rebellious child. If we were living
by Old Testament guidelines, we would take
_____ to the elders, declare the rebellious
streak, gluttony, and drinking, and then the men
of the city would stone _____ to death to
purge the evil from the community and strike godly
respect in people. Thankfully, the blood of your
Son makes this punishment void. However, your
righteous anger toward disobedience, rebellion, and
stubbornness has not changed. Please humble my
child so _____ will turn to want to please you.
(Deuteronomy 21:18–21).

Jesus came to proclaim liberty to the captives and
open prisons to those who are bound. _____
is a captive; _____ is bound. Although I am
frustrated with _____'s legal mistakes, I must
behave like the righteous person you have made
me to be. The righteous visit and care for those in
prison. I am extending godly, brotherly love when
I remember prisoners and treat them as I would
want to be treated if I were in their place. Please
communicate your love to _____ through
me. Please help me be sincerely empathetic and
let _____ accept my actions as true concern.
(Isaiah 61:1–2; Matthew 25:37–40; Hebrews 13:1–3).

Thank you for caring for _____. Please
release my child from imprisonment with a new
determination to obey the law and live as a positive
influence upon the community and the world.

In Jesus's strong name, Amen.

THE SUPPORTIVE CONNECTIONS:
WHERE TO TURN FOR ADDITIONAL HELP

When looking for resources for this chapter, I opened my search engine and typed in "What do I do if a family member gets arrested?" Pages and pages of responses popped up, many of which were from law firms. The resource below was one of the first that was not a law firm. It's a center seeking to help with the situation by giving tips to how to handle the immediate crisis.

Family Education and Resource Center—https://ferc.org/crisis/my-loved-ones-been-arrested/.

For general information about the criminal justice system, read the ample information available at the following locations online:

www.justice.gov--This is the official website of the United States Department of Justice. The Resources tab offers lots of help.

https://www.findlaw.com/criminal/criminal-law-basics/how-does-the-criminal-justice-system-work.html - This site offers easy-to-understand information about how the criminal justice system works in the United States of America.

Prison Fellowship—www.PrisonFellowship.org— Founded in 1976, the organization exists to serve all those affected by crime and incarceration and to see lives and communities restored in and out of prison—one transformed life at a time.

—CHAPTER 11—
I'M HAVING AN ABORTION

THE SIMILAR CHRONICLES: YOU ARE NOT ALONE

FRANK'S STORY

Kelly was a feminine little girl, but she was the "son" we didn't have when it came to her extracurricular preferences. This may not be politically correct now, but back when she was born, girls played with dolls and dishes, and boys played with basketballs and dirt bikes. Kelly loved sports and was good at them. She liked wearing her dresses and cute shoes on Sundays, but after school, she'd much prefer throwing a baseball or climbing a tree to playing house. She and I spent many Saturday hours and weekday late afternoons on some field or court in heavy competition.

We weren't surprised when she chose to spend time in the Peace Corps so she could, as she put it, "get my hands dirty doing work with people who need me." When she returned before her two-year stint ended, we wondered if something horrible had happened in the field. She assured us her reason for coming home was nothing like that, but she didn't want to talk about it further. She was an adult now, so we respected her privacy, but her mother and I were curious and concerned.

Kelly sulked around, no longer interested in the outdoors as she used to be. She eventually landed a job with the city. The work seemed to satisfy her, and her spunky personality began to return.

Twenty years after her mom passed away, I finally asked Kelly why she had left the Peace Corps. With bowed head and tears in her eyes, she shared she had returned because she was pregnant. She couldn't bear to disappoint her mother and me, so she had chosen to abort the baby. Kelly had lived with the pain of her decision for all those years.

Joy's Story

My oldest son's stellar high school grades and performance on placement tests worked together to present him with the glorious problem of choosing among the top universities in the nation for a college. Almost needless to say (but I'm going to say it anyway), I was tickled pink when he chose to attend an Ivy League school. After his high school graduation, at which he delivered an exciting and thoughtful valedictorian address, celebrations filled the summer.

Leaving at the end of Parent's Weekend, after I delivered him to the ivy-covered brick buildings on his new campus, was difficult. During calls home, he excitedly talked about how college was all he thought it would be and more. He was managing well in all his classes, fitting in at the dorm, meeting great new friends, and having a meaningful relationship with a wonderful girl.

Fast forward to his senior year. Suddenly, he and Angelica broke up. Since he had brought her home to meet us the year before, I had already started daydreaming, as many mothers do, about the lovely wedding they would have not long after their college graduation. He was devastated by the split, and so was I. Why? What could have happened to cause them to separate?

A few years after his college graduation, while visiting with him in his new condo, we had a long talk. I asked what happened between him and Angelica. He sighed, then told me. They had gotten pregnant during their junior year, but he had encouraged her to get an abortion. He gave her all the logical reasons—they were too young, they had no money, they weren't ready for marriage, they would have to drop out of school, their parents would freak out, and so on. Angelica went through with the abortion but could hardly live with herself afterward. Neither could he. And the shame and guilt of what they had done did not allow them to stay together.

My son had misjudged me. I would have been disappointed, but I wouldn't have freaked out if he had told me he and Angelica were expecting a baby. I know myself. Helping them decide to do the right thing and let the baby—my grandbaby—live would have quickly eclipsed my initial shock. I'm sure he'll meet and marry another wonderful young lady and Angelica will find another wonderful young man, but we'll never know what their family would and could have been.

THE STRESSFUL COMPLICATION: THE ISSUE

Abortion is a problem simply because the bumper sticker is true: In Every Abortion: One Dead, One Wounded. Women had been seeking abortions to handle unwanted pregnancies for many years, but the issue became especially problematic in 1972 for Christians in the United States when the practice became legal. "All things are lawful for me," says 1 Corinthians 6:12, "but all things are not helpful. All things are lawful for me, but I will not be brought under the power of any." Just because something is legal doesn't make it right and doesn't mean it should be condoned. However, the legality of abortion now posed another hurdle when trying to convince an emotionally distraught woman not to end an unwanted pregnancy.

Under the guise of protecting women's health, abortion advocates have worked hard to disguise the fact every abortion kills a baby. In fact, you will never see the word "baby" used in any pro-abortion literature. A baby is referred to as "the product of conception or POC." Depersonalizing the child separates the pregnant couple from the natural attachment they would have with their child as parents. Then the issue is twisted further by suggesting the POC is a threat to the woman's health.

The vast majority of abortions performed in the US are elective, not at all health related. The bottom-line reason for the murder is a baby would be an inconvenience, an embarrassment, and an interruption. I know of instances in which abortion "clinics" flat-out lied to the mothers of pregnant teens to get them to bring the girls in for abortions. Both girls had discovered their normal pregnancies at their primary doctors' offices before being taken to the abortion mill for a second opinion. In one case, the mother was told the daughter had an ectopic pregnancy and the daughter would die if the pregnancy were allowed to continue. In the second case, the young woman was pregnant with twins and the mother was told the daughter would die delivering them because she was so young.

THE SAVIOR'S COMMUNICATION: THE BIBLE'S MESSAGE

The decision to abort a pregnancy, as other life choices, must be weighed against Scripture. Does God's Word speak about abortion? Yes.

The Bible speaks of the unborn child as a living human being. As the psalmist speaks of himself in utero, Psalm 139:13–16 states plainly:

For You formed my inward parts; You covered me in my mother's womb. I will praise You, for I am fearfully *and* wonderfully made; marvelous are Your works, and *that* my soul knows very well. My frame was not hidden from You, when I was made in secret, *And* skillfully wrought in the lowest parts of the earth. Your eyes saw my substance, being yet unformed. And in Your book they all were written, the days fashioned for me, when *as yet there were* none of them.

The writer of Psalm 139 clearly understands he was a person, a living human being, even as he was forming in his mother's womb. In the Ten Commandments, we find the straightforward prohibition, "You shall not murder" (Exodus 20:13). Ending a human life is either murder or manslaughter. Manslaughter is unintentional. Murder is intentional, and first-degree murder is pre-planned "with malice aforethought." Abortion qualifies as a first-degree contract murder because it is planned, scheduled, and the "hit man"—the doctor at the clinic—is hired and paid to carry out the act.

Ending the life of a child is not the appropriate reaction to an unplanned pregnancy. Life is so precious because humankind was created in God's image. To murder a person is an attack on God's image in that person. The death penalty (see Genesis 9:6) is the ultimate punishment reserved for the lawbreaker who takes another's life. The murderer can no longer enjoy the gift of life which was stolen from another person. A human person developing inside a womb exists and deserves to become and enjoy all God has in store.

The punishment for taking an unborn life is completely unbalanced. Scott Peterson was "convicted of first-degree murder for [his wife Laci's] death, and second-degree murder for the death of their unborn son Conner." [1] But if Laci had gone to an abortion clinic and ended Conner's life on the same day before giving birth to him, she would not have received any punishment at all. The value of a life should not be based upon whether parents want the life. A life is inherently valuable regardless of the feelings of other people.

Married and unmarried women get abortions, so we are not speaking here only of single adults. When God's Word is obeyed, children are to be conceived within a marriage. The Bible tells us children are a reward even if our adult children's babies are conceived when the parents are not married. "Like arrows in the hand of a warrior, so *are* the children of one's youth. Happy *is* the man who has his quiver full of them" (Psalm 127:4–5). Once the shock of the unplanned pregnancy has passed, excitement about the new life is likely to set in, and numerous unplanned children have provided immeasurable joy to their families as well as incredible benefit to mankind.

THE SINCERE CARE-FRONTATION

How do we care for yet confront our young adult daughter who plans to have an abortion or our son who encourages his girlfriend to do so?

The challenge for parents is to de-escalate the emotions of the moment and focus on both the mental and emotional state of our kids, along with the realities of the new responsibilities now before them. Concentrate on doing what's right for all concerned, which includes the baby now, not on what's popular or politically correct or on what makes you feel better.

You can still provide care if you learn after the fact your child has had or has encouraged an abortion. The Colorado Springs Pregnancy Center has published a clear and concise article entitled "Side Effects of Abortion."[2]

This is a straightforward explanation of how each abortion procedure is performed and lists the negative side effects of each. Women having abortions are rarely offered these facts, unlike what happens dealing with other medical procedures. Offer this site to your daughter so she can at least be fully educated about what has happened to her body and her baby. She should also schedule a follow-up exam with her primary care physician to be sure nothing went wrong during the abortion procedure and none of the side effects are sneaking up on her.

The mental care of a post-abortive woman needs be a primary concern as well. According to an article on the Medical News Today website, "It is not unusual to experience a range of psychological and emotional responses. Some people may feel relief ... while others may experience a range of negative emotions ... negative feelings include guilt, anger, shame, remorse or regret ... [and even] thoughts of suicide."[3]

And don't forget about the post-abortive care for the father of the baby. They are often overlooked in this conversation, yet men also experience guilt over encouraging the abortion and may also share strong feelings of grief about their loss.

Hopefully, you will have the opportunity to walk alongside your daughter or son before the abortion takes place. Even so, the final decision belongs to your young adult. By letting you in on the problem, they are affording you a great opportunity to possibly influence the outcome of their decision.

All people want to feel fully heard. Listen to why your daughter wants to have an abortion (or why your son wants to encourage his girlfriend to do so). Let her know you want to understand her feelings and concerns. Consider asking how she is feeling physically, emotionally, and spiritually about the situation. Calmly counter her arguments. Encourage her to listen to you as patiently as you listened to her. Gently include the information discussed in the paragraphs above, but also allay her fears by opening her eyes to alternatives such as adoption, allowing a family member to raise the baby, or offering your time to help with the baby.

A positive attitude toward the new life will help both of you. Begin to talk excitedly about your new grandbaby. It's also a great idea to take your daughter to a clinic where she can get an ultrasound picture. A mother who sees her baby can rarely end its life. And while you're sharing, share the truth—raising a child can be hard and expensive. Having sex is an adult decision, so stepping up to adult consequences is an adult decision as well. Christian adults do not take the easy way out because it's convenient. The long-lasting effects of choosing an abortion can be overwhelming.

And let's be honest—lots of parents have their own story to tell. Did you have an abortion or were you tempted to have one when you were a young woman? Now's the time to share how you avoided having the abortion or how you felt after going through with it.

I honestly have no answer regarding a pregnancy that happens as the result of rape or incest. Nor do I have an answer as to the discussion of criminalizing mothers who consent and doctors who perform abortions. What I do know is what the majority of people agree about and what the legal system already handles:

- A rapist deserves punishment for violating a woman whether a pregnancy has resulted or not.

- An incestuous man (a near relative) who violates a woman against her will is, in essence, a rapist, so deserves criminal prosecution.

- Mothers who murder their children after they are born are normally arrested.

So how do we balance the logic? Rape and incest are just as wrong as killing a baby. The rapist is the criminal, not the baby, so it does not follow that the baby should receive the death penalty. And pre-born babies are just as human as children we can see outside of the womb.

No child is an accident or a mistake. The timing may be off from our perspective, but children are a reward from God, and this little one on the way is no exception.

THE SWEET COMMUNION: HOW TO PRAY

Include your child's name in the blanks in the following prayer as she considers abortion.

Dear God,

In the same way _____ is a blessing to me, I pray she/he sees this unborn baby as a blessing. You were not surprised by this pregnancy. Please move _____ to reconsider ending the life of this baby, one of your precious creations. You are forming this baby who is one of your marvelous works. You are skillfully designing everything about this child. You see this new life and you have already fashioned the days for this child (Psalm 139:13–16).

Help _____ to realize abortion ends with the death of the child. Life is precious and _____ does not want that on her conscience. Although abortion is legal in the United States of America, impress upon _____ having one is not helpful nor in your will. Please do not let _____ be brought under the power of temptation to end this child's life (Exodus 20:13, 1 Corinthians 6:12).

As parents, _____ and _____ will be warriors. This child will be an arrow in their hands, and they will be happy with him. Please choose those new parents if it will be best for the child for them to give the baby into the arms of different parents. Comfort the birth parents with your peace, and strengthen the adoptive parents with confidence, letting them all know they are doing your will for the baby (Psalm 127:4–5).

If your daughter has already had an abortion, you might pray for her this way:

Dear God,

My sweet daughter has experienced an abortion. I need for you to please comfort _____. The death of a child, especially a child still in utero, rips a part of a woman away. Heal _____ both physically and emotionally. Encourage her to turn to you with her doubts, fears, guilt, shame, pain, and grief, and help me to provide a loving shoulder for her to lean and cry on. Revive _____ spiritually and forgive her according to your boundless mercy. Let _____ know she can move forward with the wisdom learned from this episode of her life and live out a full life which will still be pleasing to you. Transform this tragic incident to make _____ wiser and a more compassionate woman.

If your son was involved with a young woman who aborted his baby, you might pray for him as follows:

Dear God,

You know my son, _____. You are aware he impregnated his lady friend, and now, she has had an abortion. Whatever role he played in the termination of this life, I plead for you to please forgive him. Visit his heart and heal it as _____ processes what has happened. Draw him to your throne. Teach _____ lessons about manhood and fatherhood to take into his future. Heal his pain, shame, guilt, fear, and grief. Strengthen him. Transform this tragic incident to make _____ wiser and help him grow spiritually.

In Jesus's strong name, Amen.

THE SUPPORTIVE CONNECTIONS:
WHERE TO TURN FOR ADDITIONAL HELP

Crisis Pregnancy Centers: All crisis pregnancy centers (CPCs) offer pregnancy tests and information. Some offer limited medical services, such as ultrasounds. There are 2525 CPCs listed on this site. Select a location to find CPCs near you. https://crisispregnancycentermap.com/

The Christian Counseling & Educational Foundation (CCEF) was founded in 1968 and exists to apply scriptural truths to modern problems. https://www.ccef.org/topic/abortion/

Dove Christian Counseling offers help as well. http://www.dovechristiancounseling.com/Abortion.html

Lifetime Adoption is a Christian domestic adoption agency. It has over thirty years of experience in building families through domestic infant adoption. https://lifetimeadoption.com/adoptive-families/

—CHAPTER 12—
I'M LIVING IN AN ABUSIVE RELATIONSHIP AND/OR I'M ABUSIVE TOWARD MY KIDS/SPOUSE

THE SIMILAR CHRONICLES: YOU ARE NOT ALONE

GENEVIE'S STORY

When our son announced his engagement, we were beyond-the-moon excited. Shelton was our only son, and we wondered if he would ever love anything more than his art. When we met Claire, we quickly understood how art took second place. She was as lovely and personable as Shelton had described, and we fell in love with her immediately. We would also soon learn she was talented and serious about her faith too.

Just before their second anniversary, we welcomed their first child, sweet little Olivia Grace, into the world. But then I received a disturbing phone call from Claire a short three months after Olivia's arrival.

"Mom," (we had become close enough for her to refer to me as Mom) "I have something very troubling to tell you. Olivia and I are over here at my mom and dad's house, and we'll be staying here for a while. Shelton got upset because I refused to butter his toast for him. He jumped up from the table, grabbed me around the neck, pushed me to the floor, and began choking me. When he got up and shut himself in our bedroom, I picked up Olivia, grabbed my purse and Olivia's diaper bag, and got out of there."

I had seen Shelton's temper cause him to slam some doors before, but I never expected he could go this far. Claire did not deserve this type of treatment. "Where is Shelton now?" I planned to give that boy a piece of my mind.

"I guess he's home. I don't know, and right now, I really don't care. I left the house and went straight to our pastor. We're leaders at our church, so before calling the police, I figured Pastor Ben could possibly talk some sense into him. I have bruises on my neck and arms. I refuse to become a battered wife who doesn't tell anyone about what's happening for twenty years. I'm not going back to him until he confesses, begs me for forgiveness, promises never to do this again, and gets counseling."

"Claire, I don't blame you. There's no excuse for manhandling his wife, the mother of his child. Wait until I get my hands on him. He'll understand what being battered is really like."

THE STRESSFUL COMPLICATION: THE ISSUE

Claire broke the cycle of abuse before it had a chance to solidify in her life. Shelton faced his anger problems, sincerely asked for Claire's forgiveness, and submitted to counseling. He and Claire were able to get back together and move forward with their marriage because of Claire's refusal to accept abusive treatment and hide the issue.

According to an article published on the website of the National Center for Biotechnology Information, U.S. National Library of Medicine, August 3, 2020, men can be victims of domestic violence; however, "the prevalence of violence against men and the risk factors for it have been little studied to date." Because of this, our comments in this chapter will focus on women as victims and men as perpetrators. However, if your adult son is the victim of domestic violence, the same precautions can be followed.[1]

Unfortunately, domestic abuse is prevalent. The National Coalition Against Domestic Violence (NCADV) lists some alarming statistics:

- One in four women (and 1 in 10 men) experience domestic violence annually.

- Two hundred seventy-three gun-related domestic violence fatalities happened in the United States in the first half of 2021 alone.

- Ten million people a year are physically abused by an intimate partner.

- Nineteen thousand calls a day are made to domestic violence hotlines.

- Intimate partner violence is most common against women 18–24.[2]

A Time.com article reported more bad news. The stress of the COVID-19 pandemic coupled with quarantine resulted in the troubling rise of physical violence perpetrated by an intimate partner.[3]

Sadly, not every woman is able to break away from domestic abuse as quickly as Claire did. Domestic abuse exists even in the church. Unfortunately, abused women frequently receive counsel from pastors or overseers to return to the abuser and submit to him as a good Christian wife should do. Even unmarried women suffer abuse at the hands of their boyfriends. Because church leadership is often patriarchal, until recent years, women did not have places to go for Christian assistance or advice unbiased from a male point of view.

Christianity Today Online tackled this issue in a comprehensive article by Brad Wilcox in December 2017. In his article is entitled "Evangelicals and Domestic Violence: Are Christian Men More Abusive?" Wilcox quotes an Australian Broadcasting Corporation (ABC) report claiming, "The church is not just failing to sufficiently address domestic violence, it is both enabling and concealing it." The report "left the impression some evangelicals' support for gender traditionalism and male headship set the stage for abusive behavior."

Although Wilcox cites research to debunk this specific claim of the ABC report, violence against women in Christian homes is still a huge problem. Wilcox admits "domestic violence is still present in church-going homes, and Christian clergy, counselors, and lay leaders need to do a much better job of articulating clear, powerful messages about abuse."[4]

As with all skeletons, the jangling bones of domestic abuse must not be hidden because of embarrassment or fear. When you become aware of your daughter being battered physically or emotionally, she must be convinced to leave this environment. Unlike our bodies' wounds, domestic abuse does not heal by itself—it only gets worse. After all, the Bible tells us, "Because the sentence against an evil work is not executed speedily, therefore the heart of the sons of men is fully set in them to do evil" (Ecclesiastes 8:11 NKJV).

THE SAVIOR'S COMMUNICATION:
THE BIBLE'S MESSAGE

The phrase "domestic violence" is not in the Bible, but that does not mean God has not communicated his will concerning it. The word "deodorant" isn't in the Bible either, but that does not mean it is against God's will for us to use it. The Bible makes abundantly clear how a husband ought to act toward his wife, and beating her up physically and berating her verbally are not consistent with God's directives.

Solomon's book of proverbs contains an overall idea about how a husband ought to relate to his wife. Proverbs 5:18–19 tells husbands, "Let your wife be a fountain of blessing for you. Rejoice in the wife of your youth ... May you always be captivated by her love (NLT).

Several verses in the New Testament give husbands specific commandments regarding the treatment God expects wives to receive. First Peter 3:7 tells husbands to "dwell with *them* with understanding, giving honor to the wife, as to the weaker vessel." And God is clear in telling husbands to steer clear of perpetrating violence upon their wives using harmful actions and words in Colossians 3:19 when Paul writes, "Husbands, love your wives and do not be bitter toward them."

I'm pretty sure breaking your wife's bones, punching her face so she gets black eyes and bruises, giving her a concussion, pulling her hair, cursing her, calling her names (using expletives like the "b" word, for example), choking, stabbing, and shooting her all qualify as harsh and bitter treatment.

And please do not forget "harsh treatment" also includes emotional abuse. One of my friends has a sister who, before she broke away, suffered tremendously in her marriage. Her husband was shrewd enough never to lay a hand on her to cause bruising or leave any other evidence of his abuse. He completely controlled her life through intimidation, deception, threats, tracking her every move, and doing everything he could to isolate and cut her off from her family and support system. The way he berated her, mocked her faith, attacked her with outrageous accusations and suspicions, and reviled her friends and family went beyond cruel—it was truly evil.

God's soul hates "the one who loves violence" (Psalm 11:5). And James, the Lord's brother, tells us we all—including husbands—are to be "slow to wrath [anger]; for the wrath [anger] of man does not produce the righteousness of God" (James 1:19–20).

Finally, in Paul's second letter to Timothy, the elder apostle informed the young preacher "that in the last days perilous times will come" including people who would have all sorts of negative characteristics. Those people would exhibit undesirable qualities including being "unloving, unforgiving, slanderers, without self-control, brutal, despisers of good," all descriptive of the behavior of a domestic abuser (2 Timothy 3:1–3).

THE SINCERE CARE-FRONTATION

Abuse is never to be tolerated, and it's not the victim's fault. Although victims are embarrassed and may deny their ability to control or escape the abuser, it is vitally important you do not remain silent. Claire told everyone immediately and refused to allow the abuse to continue and grow. She told their pastor, both sets of parents, his friends, and police officers they knew as personal acquaintances. Abusers continue in the abusive cycle until serious counseling and change can be accomplished. The life-threatening nature of domestic abuse makes addressing this issue immediately critical.

Abusers get away with their treachery because they are stronger and more formidable than the women they control. They escalate to maintain their power. They are adept at hiding their atrocious actions from others who would disapprove or stop them. Your abused daughter must be convinced she can be safe and will survive apart from him and his violent treatment. Sometimes, if her self-esteem is low, she must also be convinced she does not deserve such treatment, and she will never be able to change him.

A pastor friend of mine—we'll call him Rev. Luke—recounts a time when he discovered another pastor—we'll call him Brother Avery—was abusing his wife. Before the shocking discovery, Rev. Luke had invited Brother Avery to preach at his church. However, between the invitation and the Sunday morning he was scheduled to take the pulpit, Brother Avery had severely roughed up his wife, and the wife revealed the abuse to Rev. Luke without her husband's knowledge. So, when Brother Avery showed up to preach, Rev. Luke just had him sit through the service instead of being allowed to deliver the sermon.

After the service ended, Rev. Luke dismissed the congregation, told his deacons to give him some privacy, and invited Brother Avery to a courtyard behind the church. There, all six feet, eleven inches of Rev. Luke loomed even larger as he removed his suit coat and challenged Brother Avery to treat him like he treated his wife and see what would happen. Of course, Brother Avery's five foot, ten-inch frame was no match for Rev. Luke who pushed him around the courtyard as he begged to escape. In no uncertain terms, Rev. Luke let Brother Avery know he had abused his wife for the last time, and his reputation as a pastor was finished. Brother Avery's congregation and all the other pastors in their district denomination would know of his treachery against his wife.

Abused women are afraid to separate from their abusers because abusers have convincingly proven they will carry out their threats. Because of this, the power of the threats needs to be neutralized. Besides safely removing your daughter from the abuser, she must also be removed from other fears such as financial ruin, loss of her children, homelessness, and her husband's retribution. And don't forget, despite all, she probably loves her husband and must deal with the emotional earthquake of her broken heart.

As we deal with tough yet delicate situations such as this, Matthew 10:16 tells us to "be wise as serpents and harmless as doves." With the necessary stealth, get your daughter to a safe place. If you don't have a personal "Rev. Luke," do not be afraid to contact authorities to either remove your daughter and the children from her man's reach or press charges and have him removed from the home. Restraining orders can be put in place, but do not work if your daughter's husband or boyfriend is determined not to let her go. In an extreme case, your daughter may need to be hidden at a shelter at least for a while.

Lifeway Research lists practical ways a church can be involved when a woman needs help extricating herself from her abuser. The article suggests the following practical help:

- Is there a church member with rental property where a woman like [your daughter] and her children can stay?
- Are there coaches or counselors on staff who can help [your daughter] create a plan of action?
- Will the youth pastor and the children's minister step up to provide emotional support for the children?
- Are the elders willing to confront the husband, to help him address his issues, and work toward his emotional healing?
- Does the church have a benevolence fund to help [your daughter] pay rent, electric bills, or the cost for counseling?
- Is there a food ministry to provide meals for [your daughter] and her kids?
- Does anyone own a business needing an employee?
- Who can help [your daughter] find a job?

- Which woman who has lived through domestic abuse will come alongside [your daughter] and provide emotional support?[5]

One more thing: first, if children are involved, contact a family law attorney. The attorney will apprise your daughter of her legal rights and will help her protect them. For example, leaving her abuser can be twisted by the husband's attorney to prove she does not need the financial support for which she is asking.

Even though it may take her several times to leave her abuser, a woman suffering domestic abuse must know her family and others will be there for her no matter what. Until she is ready to make a permanent break, the people in her support system must be patient, nonjudgmental, and ready to respond on a moment's notice when she asks for help.

THE SWEET COMMUNION: HOW TO PRAY

Your daughter is in trouble, and you're beyond concerned. It's natural to want to destroy the man who is hurting her, but you realize two wrongs don't make a right. You must act with a cool head. Before you do anything, pray. Start here by inserting your daughter's name in the blanks. After you pray, listen to the Spirit's whispers, then go about the business at hand following what God is telling you to do, the way God is telling you to do it.

Dear God,

I am incredibly concerned about _____. She is in love with the man who is abusing her and I am afraid for her life. She does not seem to be able to extricate herself from his grasp. _____ is afraid.

Please Lord, start by opening _____'s eyes to the danger she is in. Help her to see the treatment this man is directing toward her is heartless, brutal, abusive, and out of control. His abuse is not the proof of his love for her. He is violent and God hates that (2 Timothy 3:1–3; Psalm 11:5).

Help _____ to believe your Word about how a man should treat her. Help her realize she is deserving of a man who finds joy in her and has earned her love. Help _____ realize a man is supposed to honor her and live with her in an understanding way, being slow to get angry. Let _____ know she deserves a man who will love her and not be harsh toward her (Proverbs 5:18–19; I Peter 3:7; James 1:19–20; Colossians 3:19).

For those of us who love _____, speak to us and guide us so we'll know how to handle this situation with wisdom. Please direct us to the correct authorities, a safe shelter, and other people who can help us. And please take the anger out of _____'s abuser. Deflate all his wrath, remove him from access to weapons, and shield _____ from him in every way. I thank you in advance for a positive outcome that frees _____ from this man, heals her physical and emotional scars, and sets her on the path to find the kind of love that will bring her true joy and contentment (Matthew 10:16).

THE SUPPORTIVE CONNECTIONS: WHERE TO TURN FOR ADDITIONAL HELP

Thanks to the internet, it is easy to find domestic violence hotlines operated by federal, state, county, city, and private agencies. As I conducted my research, I even came across a site where a pop-up directed me to a secure connection that could not be traced in the event an abuser would be trying to check up on what I had been doing online. Below are the connections to the US government sites. Hundreds more exist.

U.S. DEPARTMENT OF HEALTH AND HUMAN SERVICES

Help for Victims & Survivors of Domestic Violence
National Domestic Violence Hotline—https://www.thehotline.org/

1-800-799-SAFE (1-800-799-7233)
TTY: (800) 787-3244)

DOMESTIC OR PARTNER VIOLENCE

Violence Prevention (Centers for Disease Control and Prevention) https://www.cdc.gov/ViolencePrevention/index.html

Domestic Violence | en español (MedlinePlus®)
https://medlineplus.gov/domesticviolence.html

Shelters and Sheltering Programs that Help Women

Many women who are victims of domestic violence need emergency rescue. As with the hotline numbers, there are many women's shelters all over the United States to help your daughter. Here are only a very few along with some of the services they provide:

Bright Horizons: Advocacy and shelter services
https://brighthorizonsne.org/services/

Sheltering Wings: Emergency housing, life skills programs, children and youth services
https://shelteringwings.org/

Women's Shelters: United States and International, Women's Shelters Resources. https://www.domestic-violence-help.org/womens-shelters.html This is valuable site lists the direct contact information for many women's shelters all over the United States and in other countries.

DomesticShelters.org: This site lists the top-rated domestic violence shelters and programs.
https://www.domesticshelters.org/.

BOOK

Overcoming the Narcissist, Sociopath, Psychopath, and Other Domestic Abusers: The Comprehensive Handbook to Recognize, Remove and Recover from Abuse. Charlene D. Quint J.D. C.D.V.P., October 13, 2020

—CHAPTER 13—
I'M GETTING A DIVORCE

THE SIMILAR CHRONICLES: YOU ARE NOT ALONE

VIRGIL'S STORY

My wife and I always joked that our youngest daughter was my pleasant midlife crisis. As the senior pastor of a prominent congregation, I was careful to make choices to please God and set a good example for my family and church members. Instead of buying a sports car or spending money frivolously on some other possession that would lose its value, I convinced my wife our early forties was not too late to have another baby. Nine months later, along came Diamond. She joined her fifteen-year-old brother and ten-year-old sister.

By the time Diamond was twelve, both her brother and sister were married and out of the house. She grew into a lovely teenager, and while Diamond was a daddy's girl, she had boyfriends who periodically came by the house. I suspiciously eyed each young man, sizing them up to see if they were worthy of my precious daughter's hand. Like one of my favorite hymns says, I found, "No, not one!"

After Diamond graduated from college and started her career, she brought Douglas to meet us. This one seemed to have promise—polite, personable, charismatic, relaxed, handsome. Douglas was in his last year of seminary and was headed into the ministry. The more we got to know him, the more we liked him. He had absolutely everything going for him, but I still wondered if he would be more of a Saul than a David—head and shoulders above the rest but rotten inside rather than a man who would prove himself to be one after God's own heart. I guess no one would ever be perfect for my daughters, but I knew I had to trust their adult choices and let go.

Diamond married Douglas, but just four years in, trouble erupted in paradise. I popped over to their house for a surprise lunch visit one day and Diamond answered the door. Her black eye revealed Douglas had hit her. It was lucky for him he wasn't home. I insisted Diamond pack a few things for herself and the babies. Since the car seats were in her car, she and the kids followed me to our house. I called Douglas once they were safely with us and away from him.

I do not recommend that couples get divorced, but I wanted my Diamond to be free of this monster. Once the physical abuse was exposed, Diamond also told us, to our chagrin, about the emotional abuse she had endured. We also discovered Douglas had quit his job and was spending the money Diamond was making to help another woman care for her five children. Douglas insisted he was simply being a good pastor to assist a family in need.

It meant stepping down from her position as First Lady at their church, but I supported Diamond's decision to divorce the unrepentant Douglas on the grounds of neglect and the suspected affair. My daughter deserved much more respect. She'd find a husband after God's heart one day.

THE STRESSFUL COMPLICATION

Divorce is particularly hard on the Christian family because among people of faith, marriages are supposed to work. For ages and in many societies, marital rights were largely patriarchal, allowing the husband to divorce the wife for various (even frivolous) reasons but not the other way around. Couples entered marriage understanding it to be a lifelong commitment. Disillusionment about marriage exists today and has grown partly because of the failure rate of Christian marriages. The sentiment seems to be, "Well, if you two trust in God and your marriage can't survive, whose can? It's better not to make a commitment in the first place if the relationship is just going to end up in ruins." In relatively recent times, the culture has begun to bend the time-honored rules that have governed our understanding of the permanence of marriage.

Divorce is tough. Whether the two people in the relationship have formally married or are living together in a civil partnership, the emotional effects of the dissolution of the relationship are the same. The result leaves people broken.

A Christian family fractured by divorce damages the picture of Christ and the church marriage is supposed to represent. Divorce also creates additional multilayered problems including the separation of property, extended family drama, church membership decisions, and functioning as a single. When children are involved, the difficulties are compounded. The stepfamily spectacle can be mind-boggling as well. Not every blended family turns out to be *The Brady Bunch*.

My friend Lavinia lived through a nightmare of church membership drama when her marriage broke up. Lavinia had not considered leaving her church. She and her husband had been founding board members, and even as the congregation grew, she felt as though each person was a member of her family. Sadly, her husband had committed indiscretions with another woman and left the church. Congregants rallied around Lavinia at first, providing comfort, financial help, and assistance with her children. But when she started dating a man they didn't know, the comfort turned cold. Her church family had its own ideas about how she should live. They were used to her as they saw her with the first husband. Then they had accepted her in her neediness. However, they could not accept her life with another man. In the end, Lavinia joined a different church where there was no history to taint anyone's view of her.

It's hard to know all the minefields awaiting our children when they face the prospect of divorce. Do all you can to help the family stay together but be there for support if divorce is the ultimate choice. Keep Romans 12:18 in mind: "If it is possible, as much as depends on you, live peaceably with all men."

THE SAVIOR'S COMMUNICATION:
THE BIBLE'S MESSAGE

Before we can fully understand God's view of divorce, we must grasp his view of marriage. We hear of marriage in the Bible in Genesis, the very first book. To correct the problem of the first thing that was not good—Adam's solitary state—God set him up to realize for himself he was alone. Charged with naming all the animals, Adam took up the challenge, only to discover there was no creature on the planet who could be his helpful companion. God then performed the first surgery and fashioned Eve from one of Adam's ribs (See Genesis 2:18). When God introduced Eve to Adam, he exclaimed, "This *is* now bone of my bones and flesh of my flesh; she shall be called Woman, because she was taken out of Man" (Genesis 2:23). God then had the writer add the commentary, "Therefore a man shall leave his father and mother and be joined to his wife, and they shall become one flesh" (Genesis 2:24).

The hermeneutical principle known as the law of first mention sheds light on our quest to interpret this passage.

This principle "simply means that the very first time any important word [or doctrine] is mentioned in the Bible ... Scripture gives ... its most complete, and accurate, meaning to not only serve as a 'key' in understanding the ... Biblical concept, but to also provide a foundation for its fuller development in later parts of the Bible."[1]

So, here in Genesis 2:18–24, we learn several important principles about marriage from this first mention. First, marriage is God's idea—and all of God's ideas are good. Second, marriage is between two people. Third, those two people are to be of the two genders God created—male and female. Fourth, marriage forms a new family. Fifth, marriage is to be exclusive. And sixth, marriage is to be for life (becoming one flesh melds these two people into one).

When the Pharisees questioned Jesus about divorce, he took them back to the first mention of marriage and quoted Genesis 2:24. Based on that, he answered their question about divorce by adding, "Therefore what God has joined together, let not man separate" (Matthew 19:6 NKJV).

The Pharisees were not satisfied with Jesus's answer, so they challenged him further. The conversation continued as follows:

> They said to Him, "Why then did Moses command to give a certificate of divorce, and to put her away?"
> He said to them, "Moses, because of the hardness of your hearts, permitted you to divorce your wives, but from the beginning it was not so. And I say to you, whoever divorces his wife, except for sexual immorality, and marries another, commits adultery; and whoever marries her who is divorced commits adultery." (Matthew 19:7–9)

Note the difference between the Pharisees' word "command" and Jesus's word "permitted." Because men had been hardheaded and disobedient, God permitted divorce, but he didn't change his mind about the practice nor excuse people from the fallout.

God's feelings about divorce are clear. Malachi 2:16 says, "'For the LORD God of Israel says that He hates divorce, for it covers one's garment with violence,' says the LORD of hosts. 'Therefore take heed to your spirit, That you do not deal treacherously.'" (Dealing treacherously means spouses are not to cheat on each other.)

Marriage is also supposed to be a picture of the relationship between Christ and the church. In Paul's discussion about how husbands and wives are to relate to each other, the Holy Spirit directed him to write to the church at Ephesus:

> Wives, submit to your own husbands, as to the Lord. For the husband is head of the wife, as also Christ is head of the church; and He is the Savior of the body. Therefore, just as the church is subject to Christ, so *let* the wives *be* to their own husbands in everything. Husbands, love your wives, just as Christ also loved the church and gave Himself for her, that He might sanctify and cleanse her with the washing of water by the word, that He might present her to Himself a glorious church, not having spot or wrinkle or any such thing, but that she should be holy and without blemish. So husbands ought to love their own wives as their own bodies; he who loves his wife loves himself. For no one ever hated his own flesh, but nourishes and cherishes it, just as the Lord *does* the church. (Ephesians 5:22–29)

Biblically, the one clear detachment from marriage is the death of the spouse. The two exceptions allowing—not commanding—divorce are adultery and desertion. Proof texts supporting these statements include the following:

> "Now to the married I command, *yet* not I but the Lord: A wife is not to depart from *her* husband. But even if she

does depart, let her remain unmarried or be reconciled to *her* husband. And a husband is not to divorce *his* wife" (1 Corinthians 7:10–11).

"For the woman who has a husband is bound by the law to *her* husband as long as he lives. But if the husband dies, she is released from the law of *her* husband" (Romans 7:2).

"And I say to you, whoever divorces his wife, except for sexual immorality, and marries another, commits adultery" (Matthew 19:9).

"And a woman who has a husband who does not believe, if he is willing to live with her, let her not divorce him. For the unbelieving husband is sanctified by the wife, and the unbelieving wife is sanctified by the husband; otherwise, your children would be unclean, but now they are holy. But if the unbeliever departs, let him depart; a brother or a sister is not under bondage in such *cases.* But God has called us to peace" (1 Corinthians 7:13–15).

THE SINCERE CARE-FRONTATION

How do you care for and confront your young adult son or daughter who is going through a divorce?

When your child announces a pending divorce, close your mouth and listen. Your child will want you to take sides, but it may be both impractical and dishonest for you to do so, especially if you can see your child is holding the lion's share of blame for the break-up. Still remember there are three sides to every divorce story: your child's side, the spouse's side, and the truth.

Determine to be supportive yet honest. Function as both a shoulder to cry on and a sounding board. No matter how much you may lean for or against the divorce, respect your child's adulthood and offer advice only when specifically asked. Because of the emotionally charged nature of divorce, your child may share with you some unreasonable, irrational, and even short-sighted plans. That's the time to wisely conduct the conversation so your advice is simply one of many suggestions. Every final decision must be theirs, or you will be blamed forever for breaking up her marriage.

When our children feel close enough to us to share their side of the painful divorce story, they should respect our adult relationship with them enough to listen to our sage counsel. As the parents, we are still able to say hard truths. If our son was the one who cheated, neglected, abused, or otherwise functioned as the major culprit, we can help him come to terms with the reality his actions were the catalyst for the pending divorce. If our daughter cheated, abused, or acted in some way identifying her as the major one at fault, we can help her see how her behavior or neglect led to the break-up. Communicating hard truth does not mean we are not supportive. We can expect the best possible outcome only if we function on the foundation of truth.

A divorce can often be finalized in a relatively short period of time depending upon the laws of the state or country. The exceptions are the cases that drag on through the courts because of difficult financial or minor child issues. Our son or daughter may require our parental care-frontation for a long time after the divorce is granted. Reestablishing oneself as a single person can be difficult not only financially, but also emotionally. The longer the marriage, the more challenging the readjustment. We need to be there to talk and listen. We can watch for pitfalls our newly divorced child cannot see.

When Lavinia changed churches, she also began to make new friends who, by design, did not know her history. This was positive on one hand because people did not judge her because of her past. On the other hand, friends who had known her for some time would have been able to read when she was going in the wrong direction. Lavinia's parents had passed away before she went through the emotionally charged period immediately following her divorce. She got stuck in the riptide of a rebound relationship with an old boyfriend. Her mother could have at least reminded her why she had broken up with this guy years ago. Without her mother's wisdom, Lavinia fell right into his lies and ended up needing to extricate herself from yet another bad relationship.

The New King James Version of the Bible says, "Faithful are the wounds of a friend, but the kisses of an enemy *are* deceitful." I like how the Contemporary English Version translates the verse to say, "You can trust a friend who corrects you, but kisses from an enemy are nothing but lies." The Passion Translation is even more clear as it states, "You can trust a friend who wounds you with his honesty, but your enemy's pretended flattery comes from insincerity." When our child is facing divorce, it's time to be a parent-friend.

THE SWEET COMMUNION: HOW TO PRAY

Few experiences make it to the top of the stress list like a divorce. Feelings of failure, abandonment, fear, disillusionment, betrayal, bewilderment, and anger could all be whirling around in our children's heads and hearts as they wade through divorce's murky waters. If they ever needed someone to intercede for them in prayer, it's now. Here are some starters for petitioning God on our children's behalf.

Dear God,

Thank you for the idea of marriage. We believed _____ and (spouse's name) were made for each other, like you made Eve for Adam, back when they got married. Right now, though, _____'s marriage is not working out so well. We need you to please intervene (Genesis 2:18).

God, only you know if _____ (wife's name) has submitted to _____ (husband's name) as she would have submitted to you. Only you know if _____ (husband's name) has functioned in the home as the head of _____ (wife's name) as Christ would lead the Church.

Only you know, God, if _____ (husband's name) loved _____ (wife's name) just as Christ also loved the church and was willing to put her needs before his own. If they were not pouring into each other like this, I ask that you give them a change of heart to reboot their marriage (Ephesians 5:22–29).

God, we know you hate divorce, so you would prefer that our marriages last a lifetime. We're also thankful that your mercy and grace cover us when we fall short of your perfection. You know, God, if sexual immorality or desertion are a part of _____'s marriage story. I am asking you to first surround _____ with peace for clear thoughts to know exactly what to do and how to do it (Malachi 2:16, 1 Corinthians 7:10–11, Matthew 19:9, 1 Corinthians 7:13–15).

During this time of contemplating divorce, quiet _____'s spirit. Help _____ to lean on you for every move. Lead _____ to the right pastor, counselor, legal aid helper, or attorney who will be honest, voicing opinions and making ethical suggestions that are based on principles in line with your Word.

THE SUPPORTIVE CONNECTIONS:
WHERE TO TURN FOR ADDITIONAL HELP

Again, if your child searches "divorce help" on the internet, pages and pages of website links emerge. Each state in the United States has help centers and hotlines that can be of assistance. Here are just a few available to people wherever they may live.

Divorcehelp.com—The homepage includes links to divorce mediation, easy divorce packages, and do it yourself divorce.

Kidshelpline.com—This site exists for children to have someone to talk to when their parents are going through a divorce. https://kidshelpline.com.au/teens/issues/when-parents-separate-or-divorce

1800attorney.com—This site leads you to licensed attorneys with whom you can speak for free legal advice about divorce. http://www.1800attorney.com/free-legal-advice/

Focus on the Family is "committed to providing ... wisdom in order to help you navigate through your questions about divorce. With our help, we hope you'll find the wisdom." https://www.focusonthefamily.com/get-help/divorce.

https://www.focusonthefamily.com/marriage/divorce-and-separation

Remember your church or a nearby church may also have counseling centers for assistance with divorce issues. Christian counselors and therapists are also listed online and work with you locally. Research therapists in your state.

—CHAPTER 14—
I HAVE AN EMOTIONAL PROBLEM OR MENTAL DISORDER

THE SIMILAR CHRONICLES: YOU'RE NOT ALONE

Sometimes the things we didn't see coming are problems thrust upon our children by heredity, an accident, or some trauma from without. Such is the case with emotional problems and mental disorders. The American Psychological Association explains the difference. An emotional problem (disorder) is defined as "any psychological disorder characterized primarily by maladjustive emotional reactions that are inappropriate or disproportionate to their cause."[1] A mental illness (disorder) is defined as "any condition characterized by cognitive and emotional disturbances, abnormal behaviors, impaired functioning, or any combination of these. Such disorders cannot be accounted for solely by environmental circumstances and may involve physiological, genetic, chemical, social, and other factors."[2] A stranglehold of shame often grips those touched by emotional problems and mental illness. Exposure kills the stigma paving the way for understanding, education, and healing to begin. God used openness and honesty to help me understand and be healed of worry and pain over my son Matthew's diagnosis. Here's the rest of my story I mentioned briefly in chapter six.

My Story

Even though Matthew was my first born, I didn't cry once we had him settled in his college dorm room and drove away. I still had one kid at home, and Matthew would be easy to get to if necessary since he was only forty-five minutes away. It felt like he was only on a sleepover. Life returned to normal minus the occasional arguments that sometimes issued forth from the bedroom he and Mark no longer shared.

Then came the fateful day we attended one of Matthew's films screened on his college campus. His actions were strange during the question-and-answer time that followed. He was jumpy, talking fast, using lots of confusing hand gestures, and was wrapped up in his hoodie like he was hiding from the audience. He was not his usual controlled, personable self. Family members frowned back and forth at each other wondering what was going on.

Over the next few weeks, I had several troubling phone calls from Matthew. He would call in a great mood, and then a few days later he'd call sounding down and depressed. He started having minor trouble with his car, but instead of getting it fixed, he traded it in—his high school graduation present—for a more expensive one. Now he had a car note and no job. What was he thinking? My husband James (Matthew's stepdad) was completely outdone and was ready to write Matthew off as utterly irresponsible and downright disrespectful.

Then we got a call from the school, but it wasn't Matthew. His dorm mates called to alert us Matthew had been taken to the hospital. He had some kind of emotional breakdown and couldn't regain his calm or composure, so they called an ambulance.

My husband and I raced to the hospital where we found him in an emergency room bed, curled up in the fetal position facing the wall. When we entered, James went around to the side of the bed where Matthew could see him. Matthew threw his arms around him, weeping and hugging him as if he were being rescued from drowning. This was the beginning of our understanding of what was really going on with Matthew. He wasn't trying to be "utterly irresponsible and downright disrespectful," he was suffering from a mental illness—bipolar disorder.

Thankfully, the college had a School of Psychology and resources to enable us to receive a correct diagnosis quickly, and Matthew was blessed to be prescribed a medication to control his symptomatic mood swings and erratic behavior.

More than ten years have passed. Not only does Matthew enjoy a successful and productive life, but we have also seen how God's hand has entrusted him with bipolar disorder for a larger, kingdom purpose. We'll talk more about that in the Care-frontation section of this chapter.

THE STRESSFUL COMPLICATION: THE ISSUE

Be it a mental illness or an emotional problem, from what I've seen and heard there are four reasons these disturbances are not more correctly diagnosed and properly treated: ignorance, misinformation, misdiagnoses, and embarrassment. Christian families are no exception in reacting to and treating our adult children poorly when it comes to mental and emotional imbalance. These challenges are just as real as physical illnesses: the pain and suffering are real.

Ignorance tops the list of why we have problems reaching out effectively to those suffering with mental illness and/or emotional imbalance. What we don't know can indeed hurt us. We react in all the wrong ways when we are ignorant about anything. People used to think those clear plastic bags from the cleaners were okay to give to little kids to play with until we discovered they are a smothering hazard. Now we're very careful to place those bags far out of a child's reach. Asbestos was used for years in building material. Now we know breathing in asbestos is extremely hazardous and an expensive abatement team must show up when it's discovered in a home to remove it safely. We respond differently toward mental illness and other verified emotional problems when we erase our ignorance about them.

Misinformation hurts us maybe more than ignorance does. At least with ignorance, we are clear we don't know something. When we are misinformed, we think we know and that makes us dangerous. We go about confidently believing our misinformation, acting on it, and even spreading it as if it were the truth. Misinformation solidifies our prejudices and impatience toward people with emotional imbalance and pain. We will believe stereotypes and even be prone to name-calling, saying things like, "So-and-so is crazy!"

Misdiagnoses are also common when dealing with people suffering with mental and emotional pain because so many variables are involved. For example, a season of grief will begin if a close family member dies. Only a trained doctor or counselor will be able to discern whether the prolonged sadness is just that person's makeup or if it has become clinical depression. We can be quick to project onto our adult child our personal diagnosis. We may dismiss a deep problem with phrases like, "Oh, he's just going through a phase," or "Give him time; he'll snap out of it," or "He's always been super sensitive," or my personal favorite (sarcasm indicated here), "He's just trying to get attention."

Finally, we don't get effective help for mental and emotional suffering because we're embarrassed. In our hearts we say, "I don't want anyone to know my child is psycho." We've made a judgment and have given up hoping against hope our child will just grow out of it or eventually get over it. We hope we can get through the next family gathering without an "incident" we'll have to explain.

Ignorance, misinformation, misdiagnoses, and embarrassment. None of these states are healthy or helpful. You didn't see this problem coming with your adult child, but here it is. Does God say anything about it?

THE SAVIOR'S COMMUNICATION: THE BIBLE'S MESSAGE

Mental and emotional distress is mentioned in the Bible by description, and there are too many references to list here. The great news is God's comfort accompanies the descriptions of emotional distress in the Bible.

The apostle Paul wrote to Timothy and us, "For God has not given us a spirit of fear, but of power and of love and of a sound mind" (2 Timothy 1:7). We easily apply this admonition to many areas of life, but we must remember this applies to mental distress as well. Fear effects our strength, our emotions, and our thinking. God intends for our minds to function clearly, our emotions to be centered in love, and our being to be strong enough to weather the storms life throws our way.

Speaking of emotional distress, Psalm 34:17–19 ensures us, "*The righteous* cry out, and the LORD hears, and delivers them out of all their troubles. The LORD *is* near to those who have a broken heart and saves such as have a contrite spirit. Many *are* the afflictions of the righteous, but the LORD delivers him out of them all."

Pretty self-explanatory, right? Being brokenhearted and crushed in spirit are not strange experiences because life deals us lots of afflictions. Even so, God has our backs. We can exhale and allow our emotions to settle as we trust in our God who is able to deliver his children from any and everything that is out to demolish our confidence and hope!

We read John 16:33 and discover that in Jesus, we "may have peace." Even though "in the world [we] will have tribulation," God encourages us to "be of good cheer." Why? Because he has "overcome the world."

So, how do we access God's power, love, and peace? How do we take heart, avoid what will crush our spirit, and experience deliverance? We must get into the habit of handing our mental and emotional distress over to Jesus. This is easier said than done, but it's the answer. First Peter 5:7 cannot be stated any more clearly, "Casting all your care upon Him, for He cares for you."

THE SINCERE CARE-FRONTATION

We may have thought we were out of the childcare business when our precious cargo celebrated their wonderful eighteenth birthday, but alas, we didn't see it coming when an adult-onset issue occurs. Discovering our young adult has an emotional or mental disorder feels like a sucker punch in the stomach. Our child is in no way to blame, and now some symptoms are manifesting as coping mechanisms try to kick in. How do we care for and confront our beloved child who tries to function as a mature individual, yet struggles in one of these areas?

The first way to practice care-frontation for our adult child who struggles with an emotional issue is to treat the diagnosis as what it is—an illness that needs to be healed like a broken arm, or an emotional problem too heavy to carry. We don't doubt the need for medical attention when our child has a broken limb. We also have no problem with the fact our child cannot function as usual at least for a while. The limb may need to be used slightly differently from now on depending upon how drastic the break is and how it had to be set. Mental illness and emotional problems demand the same respect we'd give a broken arm.

The second way to practice care-frontation is to get medical professionals involved immediately. Don't wait thinking *this is just a phase*, or *we can wait this out until it blows over*. Broken arms don't go away, and if left alone, they heal incorrectly. Ignored conditions such as bipolar, eating disorders, self-harm, or clinical depression don't go away by themselves or if left alone. If ignored, they "set" incorrectly, leading to greater dysfunction or dangerous behavior.

Care-frontation can take place a third way when we are patient with the learning curve. We need to give ourselves time to figure out what's happening and why. Short of a miraculous healing of the disorder, syndrome, or condition, this will not go away overnight, so we can stop acting like it will and give ourselves grace.

The fourth care-frontation piece is involvement in your child's treatment if you are allowed. The wrench in the works is the fact your child is an adult. Matthew recognized something was very wrong and told the people at college, "Call my momma." That is not the case in every instance. One of my friends shared that her twenty-something son invited her to his professional visits at first, but later revoked permission. Only after his third attempt to take his life did he want her to be a part of the process again.

If your child is not open to your help, you did nothing wrong. There is nothing wrong with your family. Just as our children's height, hair color, and talents are a part of their natural makeup, so are our children's other issues such as asthma, allergies, and yes, mental illnesses and possibly the predispositions to emotional disorders. I didn't wring my hands and smote my breast about Mark's asthma—I simply purchased inhalers. Why would I berate myself about Matthew's mental illness? My job is to rely on God for healing and help deal with both. Refuse to drown in blame. Instead, grab onto the life preservers who are God and other parents like me who are where you are.

If your child refuses your participation, ramp up your prayers surrounding them—never forget the power of prayer. However, if your child does allow your involvement, watch videos about the disorder and discuss how the depiction is like or unlike your case. I remember going to a psychiatrist's office with Matthew as he was interviewing doctors. The secretary seated us in the man's office where we had a few moments waiting for him to arrive. If the clutter on his desk reflected his mind, we were in the wrong place. Matthew and I laughed about the possibility of having a psychiatrist who was just as confused as the bipolar patients he was supposed to help. Matthew selected a different doctor.

Because Matthew was open with me about his difficulties, God helped me help him to settle into the routine of taking his meds. Many times, people with schizophrenia or bipolar disorder feel terrible about the prospect of taking medication for the rest of their lives. When Matthew hit that wall, the Holy Spirit gave me a great metaphor.

I said, "Matthew, you and I wear glasses. We wear them every day because we cannot see clearly without them. We never think about wearing glasses as a negative thing because we appreciate seeing clearly. Your bipolar meds are like glasses for your brain. You take that little pill every day because you want to think clearly."

Matthew responded, "Oh yeah," and has not had an issue taking his meds since.

The fourth way to practice care-frontation is to stop speaking of the disorder in hushed tones. Be upfront and open about it. This helps everyone identify trigger points.

My pastor reminds us God won't fix what we won't face. He won't heal what we won't reveal. As you start talking about what you're going through, you'll find—as I did when I started writing this book—you are not alone. You will also take the smothering power away from the situation. You'll gain control of your life rather than continuing to let the illness or the disorder control you.

I spoke earlier about how God's hand has entrusted Matthew with bipolar disorder for a larger, kingdom purpose. Well, the fifth way to participate in care-frontation is to let God use what you're learning to help others. One of Matthew's colleagues confided in him his mother was having a really hard time because his little brother was recently diagnosed with bipolar disorder. Matthew shared his own diagnosis and then offered to have me talk to his friend's mom. So, one afternoon, I sat comfortably in my den and had a long conversation with this woman I didn't even know, informing her of what I knew about bipolar disorder, comforting and encouraging her she could make it.

Another incident in which we saw how God's hand moved because of Matthew's bipolar disorder happened on a flight as I returned from a conference. A lady got on the plane crying and sat next to me. We said our hellos and exchanged names. I soon discovered that Lisa was flying to Los Angeles to pick up her son who had started self-medicating with alcohol to cope with his bipolar disorder. I excitedly told her my son had bipolar disorder too.

My reaction was the opposite of what Lisa expected, so I explained although Matthew had it, we had found an answer because we trusted God for the remedy. Our conversation opened the reality she hadn't thought much about God or Jesus Christ in relation to this problem. Long story short, by the end of the flight, she had accepted Christ and had a new outlook on how to deal with her son.

As we deplaned, Lisa was crying a different kind of tears. She hugged me and said, "I thought I was getting on this plane to go get my son out of school and see the end of his college career. Now I know I got on this plane to meet you."

"Oh no," I responded. "You got on this plane to meet Jesus."

I called Matthew as soon as I got home to tell him God had entrusted him with bipolar disorder for at least one more reason—so Lisa could be saved. Suppose God said the following to you and your child:

"Listen, my children. I need your help. I need to give you a mental illness or emotional problem because I'm trying to win someone to me. I will walk you through the problem and then I'll let you meet that person. Can I trust you to accept this problem in order to release that other person from the grip of hell?"

As God works with you and your child to understand, heal, and deliver you in and from the mental illness or emotional issue you face, let God use your journey to help others for his glory.

Finally, you may think you will find understanding within the walls of your church or from other Christians. Hopefully, that will be the case. However, I've heard very sad stories about how some churches have not caught up with the education that exists about mental illness and emotional problems. These institutions believe mental illness is the result of sin and treat families dealing with it as pariahs. One friend shared her family left the church they had attended all their lives because they were told of their daughter, "If she'd confess *all* of her sin" or "If she would pray more, she wouldn't be this way." The attitude was turned on them as parents too when it was suggested that "if Dad would read the Bible aloud more often, the problem would go away."

The church is God's idea so it's a perfect institution made up of imperfect people. Don't allow this type of ignorance to separate you from the love of the family of God. It may be best for you to start attending a church where the people have learned to embrace each other, realizing we all need each other at one time or another.

THE SWEET COMMUNION: HOW TO PRAY

God has your back as you face unexpected issues like bipolar disorder, self-harm, or eating disorders in your adult child's life. Place your child's name in the blanks below and use these verses as prayer starters.

Dear God,

I am crying out for help for _____ because my child is in trouble. _____ trouble is a crushed spirit because of the difficulty of coping with emotional and mental pain. I know you hear me when I cry out to you. Even though _____ may have a lot ahead to face, I trust you to deliver _____ from every facet of this problem. I am giving my anxiety about this to you. I ask that you help _____ do the same, knowing that you care about what touches my child (Psalm 34:17–19; I Peter 5:7).

As _____ deals with this unexpected disorder or condition, I ask you give a sound mind. Thank you for removing the spirit of fear because it does not come from you. Help _____ operate in your power and in your love (2 Timothy 1:7).

We're aware there will be trouble in this world, but this problem is really a tough one to handle. Remind _____ you have this under control. _____ can take heart, buck up, and walk with head held high because we are in league with you— the one who has overcome the world. Hold _____ *tight, eradicating the possibility of lost hope. Yes, this problem is real, and its pain is ravishing _____'s body and soul, so please continue to renew my child's inner being every day. (John 16:33; 2 Corinthians 4:16). I ask for ultimate and complete healing.*

In the strong name of Jesus, Amen.

THE SUPPORTIVE CONNECTIONS: WHERE TO TURN FOR ADDITIONAL HELP

Again, the internet is an excellent source of information and health care providers for any of the illnesses, disorders, and syndromes mentioned in this chapter. Below are just a few for starters.

For help with bipolar disorder, The American Psychiatric Society has a site filled with questions and answers, patient stories, blog posts and more. https://www.psychiatry.org/patients-families/bipolar-disorders. There are also local centers where you and your child can get the help you need. An example of one in California is Seasons in Malibu offering world class mental health treatment. https://seasonsbeachcottage.com/about/.

If your child is involved in **self-harm**, The National Alliance on Mental Illness (NAMI) offers a page on its website dedicated to giving information about this subject. https://www.nami.org/About-Mental-Illness/Common-with-Mental-Illness/Self-harm.

For help with eating disorders, The Eating Recovery Center in Colorado is an example of an organization that has a site that offers a quiz and a confidential assessment along with the information on eating disorders.

Clinical Depression is covered extensively on the Mayo Clinic's site. https://www.mayoclinic.org/diseases-conditions/depression/symptoms-causes/. PsychCentral. com (https://psychcentral.com/blog/7-ways-to-manage-clinical-depression#1 posts "7 Ways to Manage Clinical Depressions" and offers a wide variety of blog posts about many sub-topics about depression.

Talkspace.com offers a hotline to a therapist for any mental, emotional, or psychological difficulty. The great thing about Talkspace.com (https://try.talkspace.com/) is the convenience. This site allows your child to search for a therapist with whom they feel comfortable. Then your child can talk with the therapist whenever necessary.

The National Alliance on Mental Illness (NAMI) and Depression and Bipolar Support Alliance (DBSA) both serve the consumer (term used in mental health for the person with the illness) and family members. NAMI recognizes the faith component of recovery with FaithNet – https://www.nami.org/Get-Involved/NAMI-FaithNet

Mental Health Ministries (http://www.mentalhealthministries.net/) serves faith communities.

Book

Grace for the Afflicted by Matthew S. Stanford, PhD. IVP Press, 2017

ABOUT THE AUTHOR

"Live significantly!" That's the inspiring message of Sharon Norris Elliott: author, speaker, Bible teacher, editor, consultant, licensed minister, and literary agent. She writes challenging yet encouraging books in several genres including women's nonfiction, parenting, devotional, and children's literature. Her most recent women's title, *A Woman God Can Bless*, launched from Harambee Press in 2020. Elk Lake has contracted her seven-book children's *I Really Need to Know* series.

God's goodness has brought Sharon from Compton, CA, to standing before great audiences. She's a cum laude graduate of Biola University, holder of a Doctor of Theology Degree, and member of ACE, AWSA, and SCBWI. She is also a religious broadcaster on HSBN.tv, CWWN.tv, Spotify, and other social media outlets. She is founder and CEO of Life That Matters Ministries; AuthorizeMe® Literary Firm LLC; and Milk & Honey Life Retreats. Sharon serves as co-director of West Coast Christian Writers' Conference, and a member of the ministerial staff for her home congregation at Christ Second Baptist Church, Long Beach, CA.

She and her husband James live in Southern California and enjoy their church, their children, and their grandchildren.

Connect with Sharon on TikTok, Instagram, and Facebook; enjoy her devotional blog "A Heart for the Word;" and surf her website at www.AuthorizeMe.net to subscribe to her newsletter and find information about how she can help you write your book!

Here are her links:

Facebook Page https://www.facebook.com/SaneWriter/

Instagram: https://www.instagram.com/AuthorizeMeNow/

Twitter: https://twitter.com/Sanewriter

TikTok: https://www.tiktok.com/@sanewriter

LinkedIn: Dr. Sharon Elliott

ENDNOTES

CHAPTER 1

1. Martin Luther King Jr., "I Have a Dream Speech Text." *Huffington Post.* (Updated January 15, 201). https://www. huffpost.com/entry/i-have-a-dream-speech-text-martin-luther-king-jr_n_1207734.

CHAPTER 2

1. Sharon Jayson, "Unplanned Pregnancies in States Reach 4 in 10." *USA Today* (May 19, 2011). https://populationissuesnetwork.blogspot.com/2011/08/unplanned-pregnancies-in-states-reach-4.html.

2. Joyce A. Martin, M.P.H., Brady E. Hamilton, PhD, et. al.,"National Vital Statistics Report," U.S. Department of Health and Human Services (November 3, 2011), http://www.cdc.gov/nchs/data/nvsr/nvsr60/nvsr60_01.pdf.

3. Matthew Henry "Psalm 127," *Matthew Henry's Commentary on the Whole Bible Vol. 3,* (England: 1706).

CHAPTER 3

1. Nathaniel Hawthorne, "The Minister's Black Veil," *The Token and Atlantic Souvenir,* edited by Samuel Goodrich, (Boston, MA: 1836).

2. Hawthorne, "Black Veil."

3. Phil Hickey, PhD, "Homosexuality: The Mental Illness that Went Away," *Behaviorism and Mental Health*, (October 8, 2011). https://www.behaviorismandmentalhealth.com/2011/10/08/homosexuality-the-mental-illness-that-went-away/.

4. Louis and Melissa McBurney, "Christian Sex Rules: A Guide to What's Allowed in the Bedroom," *Today's Christian Woman*, (September 2008). https://www.todayschristianwoman.com/articles/2008/september/christian-sex-rules.html.

5. James Vincent, "Largest Ever Study into the Gay Gene Erodes the Notion that Sexual Orientation is a Choice," *Independent*. (November 21, 2014). https://www.independent.co.uk/news/science/largest-ever-study-gay-gene-erodes-notion-sexual-orientation-choice-9875855.html.

6. Definition of Terms, UC Berkeley-Division of Equality and Inclusion, accessed September 6, 2022. https://cejce.berkeley.edu/geneq/resources/lgbtq-resources/definition-terms.

5. Lori Wildenberg, "Bruce Jenner, Chaz Bono, and my Oldest Daughter," *Eternal Moments*. (June 15, 2015), https://loriwildenberg.com/2015/06/15/bruce-jenner-chaz-bono-and-my-oldest-daughter.

Chapter 4

1. "Warning Signs," The American Foundation for Suicide Prevention," accessed September 14, 2021, https://afsp.org/risk-factors-protective-factors-and-warning-signs#warning-signs.

2. "Behavior," https://afsp.org/risk-factors-protective-factors-and-warning-signs#warning-signs.

3. "Moods," https://afsp.org/risk-factors-protective-factors-and-warning-signs#warning-signs.

4. Corrie ten Boom and John and Elizabeth Sherrill, *The Hiding Place,* Chosen Books, (1971).

5. Dr. Ab Abercrombie, "A Biblical Response to Mental Illness and Suicide: What Should We Conclude ..." Biblical Counseling Institute, April 9, 2013, https://bcinstitute.com/a-biblical-response-to-mental-illness-and-suicide-what-should-we-conclude/.

6. Mayo Clinic Staff, "Suicide: What to do when someone is suicidal," Mayo Foundation for Medical Education and Research (MFMER), https://www.mayoclinic.org/diseases-conditions/suicide/in-depth/suicide/art-20044707.

7. "Suicide." Mayo Foundation

CHAPTER 5

1. Lydia Anderson and Zachary Scherer, "See How Marriage and Divorce Rates in Your State Stack Up," United States Census Bureau, (December 7, 2021), accessed December 21, 2021, https://www.census.gov/library/stories/2020/12/united-states-marriage-and-divorce-rates-declined-last-10-years.html.

2. Scott Stanley, "Premarital Cohabitation is Associated with Greater Odds of Divorce," Institute for Family Studies, (October 17, 2018), https://ifstudies.org/blog/premarital-cohabitation-is-still-associated-with-greater-odds-of-divorce.

3. Lawdepot.com offers a Cohabitation Agreement. https://www.lawdepot.com/contracts/cohabitation-agreement/?loc=US&ldcn=cohab#.YxYBm_HMKDU.

CHAPTER 6

1. "A Teen's Brain Isn't Fully Developed Until Age 25," Paradigm Treatment Centers, LLC., (February 23,

2021), https://paradigmtreatment.com/teens-brain-fully-developed-age/.

2. Mary McMahon, "Why Are Some Teachers Prohibited from Grading in Red Ink," Wise Geek. (August 10, 2022), https://www.wisegeek.com/why-are-some-teachers-prohibited-from-grading-in-red-ink. htm; Dan Sanchez. "What the Self-Esteem Movement Got Disastrously Wrong." Foundation for Economic Education: FEE Stories. (May 15, 2017). https://fee. org/articles/what-the-self-esteem-movement-got-disastrously-wrong/.

3. Jim Schleckser, "Nelson Mandela's Secret to Winning," Inc. (July 21, 2016), https://www.inc.com/jim-schleckser/nelson-mandela-s-secret-to-winning.html.

CHAPTER 7

1. "10 Great Reasons to Get Your College Degree," Post University Blog, (May 7, 2020) https://post.edu/blog/10-great-reasons-to-get-your-college-degree/.

CHAPTER 8

1. Bill Chappell, "Judge Backs N.Y. Parents, Saying Their 30-year-old Son Must Move Out," NPR, (May 23, 2018), https://www.npr.org/sections/thetwo-way/2018/05/23/613616315/judge-backs-n-y-parents-saying-their-30-year-old-son-must-move-out.

2. Catherine Shoichet, "52% of Young Adults in the US Are Living With Their Parents That's the Highest Share Since the Great Depression," CNN. (Updated September 4, 2020), https://www.cnn.com/2020/09/04/us/children-living-with-parents-pandemic-pew/index.html.

3. Sharon Norris Elliott, *Boomerangs to Arrows: A Godly Guide for Launching Young Adult Children*, Valley Forge: Judson Press, (2013).

4. Michelle Cox and Rene Gutteridge, *Just 18 Summers,* Stream, Il.: Tyndale House Publishers, (2014).

CHAPTER 9

1. McGovern, Patrick E., Juzhong Zhang, Jigen Tang, et al. "Fermented Beverages of Pre- and Proto-Historic China," Proceedings of the National Academy of Science, (December 8, 2004), https://www.pnas.org/doi/full/10.1073/pnas.04079211022.

2. Philip P. Kabusta, "Greek-English, s.v. pharmakeia," *The King James Bible Dictionary*, (2012), New Covenant Press, http://kingjamesbibledictionary.com/StrongsNo/g5331.

3. "Alcohol: A Short History," Foundation for a Drug-Free World, accessed December 21, 2021, https://www.drugfreeworld.org/drugfacts/alcohol/a-short-history.html.

4. "Making Decisions Regarding Tobacco Use," R. J. Reynolds Tobacco, accessed February 10, 2022, https://rjrt.com/tobacco-use-health/public-health-information/.

5. Ian Young, "6 Ways to Convince an Alcoholic/Addict to Accept Help," Sober Services, (October 24, 2014), https://www.sober-services.com/6-ways-to-convince-an-alcoholic-addict-to-accept-help/

CHAPTER 10

1. "Prison Reform: Reducing Recidivism by Strengthening the Federal Bureau of Prisons," Department of Justice Archives, accessed June 8, 2021, https://www.justice.gov/archives/prison-reform.

2. Department of Justice Archives, "Prison Reform."

CHAPTER 11

1. "Murder of Laci Peterson," accessed May 16, 2021, https://en.wikipedia.org/wiki/Murder_of_Laci_Peterson.

2. "Specific Abortion Procedures and Possible Side Effects of Abortion," Colorado Springs Pregnancy Center, accessed March 8, 2022, https://www.cspregnancycenter.com/side-effects-of-abortion.htm.

3. Karen Gepp, "Depression after Abortion: Risk Factors and How to Cope," MedicalNewsToday, (Updated April 12, 2022) https://www.medicalnewstoday.com/articles/313098.

Chapter 12

1. Verena Kolbe and Andreas Buttner, "Domestic Violence Against Men—Prevalence and Risk Factors," Aerzteblatt.DE International, (August 3, 2020), https://www.aerzteblatt.de/int/archive/article/214902.

2. "National Statistics," The National Coalition Against Domestic Violence, accessed August 7, 2021, https://ncadv.org/statistics.

3. Jeffrey Kluger, "Domestic Violence Is a Pandemic Within the COVID-19 Pandemic," *Time*, (February 3, 2021), https://time.com/5928539/domestic-violence-covid-19/.

4. Brad Wilcox, "Evangelicals and Domestic Violence: Are Christian Men More Abusive?" *Christianity Today*, (December 11, 2017), https://www.christianitytoday.com/ct/2017/december-web-only/evangelicals-domestic-violence-christian-men-domestic-abuse.html.

5. RJ Thesman, "5 Myths the Church Often Believes about Domestic Violence," Lifeway Research, (October 25, 2018), https://lifewayresearch.com/2018/10/25/5-myths-the-church-often-believes-about-domestic-violence/

Chapter 13

1. "The Law of First Mention—What is It?," NetBibleStudy.com, accessed July 30, 2022, http://netbiblestudy.com/00_cartimages/thelawoffirstmention.pdf.

CHAPTER 14

1. "Emotional Disorder," *APA Dictionary of Psychology,* American Psychological Association, accessed September 7, 2022, https://dictionary.apa.org/emotional-disorder

2. "Mental Disorder," *APA Dictionary of Psychology,* American Psychological Association, accessed September 7, 2022, https://dictionary.apa.org/mental-disorder

OTHER SHARON NORRIS ELLIOTT BOOKS

PICTURE BOOKS
I REALLY NEED TO KNOW SERIES

Why I Get into Trouble

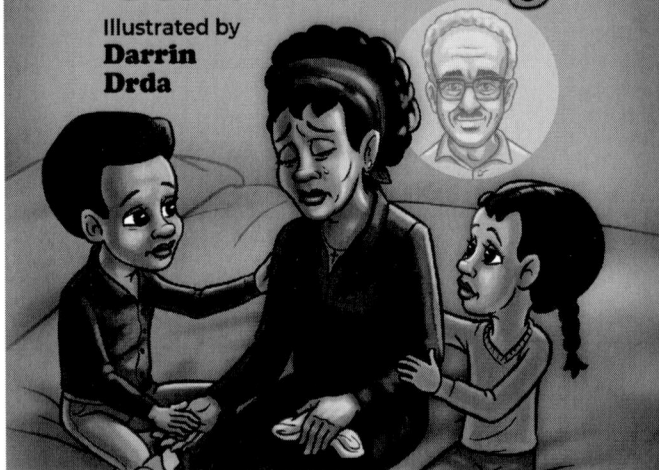

Manufactured by Amazon.ca
Acheson, AB

11099280R00125